HARROGATE IN 100 DATES

ROBERT WOODHOUSE

T0347635

The
History
Press

First published 2014

The History Press
The Mill, Brimscombe Port
Stroud, Gloucestershire, GL5 2QG
www.thehistorypress.co.uk

British Library Cataloguing in Publication Data.
A catalogue record for this book is available from the British Library.

ISBN 978 0 7524 8631 4

Typesetting and origination by The History Press
Printed in Great Britain

Contents

Introduction & Acknowledgements

It is believed that the name Harrogate is derived from the Anglo-Norse *Here-gatte*, meaning 'the way to the hill of the soldier', and it appears as a place name within the Forest of Knaresborough before settlements grew up around it. High Harrogate was at the junction of major routes and had a chantry chapel by 1400, but it is thought that Low Harrogate did not develop until some point in the sixteenth or seventeenth century.

Members of these small communities were mainly employed in agriculture but, in 1571, William Slingsby's discovery of Tewit Well heralded a major change in Harrogate's fortunes. Travellers diverted their routes to sample the waters and doctors proclaimed the value, in health terms, of a visit to 'The English Spaw' as it was termed by Dr Edmund Deane. In 1631, Michael Stanhope discovered a chalybeate or iron spring about half a mile from the Tewit Well and by 1700, Harrogate had achieved prominence as a spa.

Early accommodation for visitors was provided by local farmers but 1687 saw the opening of High Harrogate's first major hotel, the Queen, which was sited midway between the Tewit Well and St John's Well. It was soon followed by the Granby, while Low Harrogate's first hotel, the Crown, was opened in about 1700. During the 1760s Mrs Wilks, owner of the Granby Hotel, opened a theatre in a barn beside Granby Farm for the entertainment of visitors.

In 1778 a group of commissioners made an Award which defined the boundaries of Harrogate Stray, an area designated as a public common, between the settlements of High and Low Harrogate.

An increasing number of visitors were soon able to visit a new theatre and, from 1793, races on the High Stray.

A rapid increase in Harrogate's population during the first decade of the nineteenth century saw the total reach about 1,500 by 1810. During this year, a workhouse to accommodate homeless paupers was opened on the road to Starbeck. Provision of luxurious standards of bathing, with medical supervision, was further improved by the construction of premises such as Victoria Baths (1832) and Crown Baths (1834). In 1841, legislation enabled townspeople to elect twenty-one 'improvement commissioners' and there was a considerable amount of opposition to the arrival of a railway link before the opening of Brunswick station on 20 July 1848.

Harrogate's continued growth during the mid-nineteenth century is reflected by an increase in population from 3,372 in 1841 to 6,675 in 1871. The town was in celebratory mood for the delivery of a Charter of Incorporation on 6 February 1884 and again during summer 1887 to mark Queen Victoria's Golden Jubilee.

The opening of the Kursaal (later renamed the Royal Hall) brought performances by a succession of world-famous celebrities and the mysterious appearance of Agatha Christie at the Old Swan Hotel in 1926 made headline news, but the 1930s saw a rapid decline in numbers of visitors to Harrogate. The second half of the twentieth century, though, saw Harrogate's re-emergence as a conference and exhibition centre, with venues such as the International Centre. This trend has continued into the twenty-first century, with the arrival of the Tour de France in 2014, the first time the world-famous race has visited the North of England.

N.B. The Julian calendar was in use until Wednesday, 2 September 1752. The following day the Gregorian calendar was adopted, making the date Thursday, 14 September 1752. The dates in this book before and after the shift correspond to the respective calendars.

References for extracts appear at the end of each entry, and a full bibliography appears at the end of the book. All Internet sources are correct at the time of writing.

I am indebted to my wife, Sally, for her research and unstinting support and to Liz Taylorson for her administrative skills. My gratitude also goes to Bob Eastwood for information relating to railways in the Harrogate area, and the staff at Northallerton and Harrogate libraries.

Robert Woodhouse, 2014

HARROGATE
IN 100 DATES

1665

4 June

An entry in the diary of Lady Verney on this day records her impressions of conditions at a Harrogate inn:

> … We arrived at the nasty Spaw, and have now began to drinke the horrid sulfer watter, which allthough as bad as is poasable to be immajaned, yet in my judgement plesent to all the doings we have within doors. The House and all that is in it being horidly nasty, and crowded up with all sorte of company, which we eate with in a roome, as the spiders are ready to drop into my mouth, and it sure hathe nether been well cleaned nor ared this dousen years; it makes me much moore sick than the nasty watter.

The publication of *Spadacrene Anglica* (The English Spa) by Dr Edmund Deane in 1626 led to a considerable increase of visitors to the locality, where the villages of High and Low Harrogate were separated by open fields. During the summer months, local farmers provided accommodation for visitors to the spa and supplied their dietary needs from home-grown produce. In the latter years of the seventeenth century, some farmhouses were even properly converted into inns as High Harrogate, with its mineral springs, became more fashionable than Low Harrogate's 'stinking wells'.

Neesam, Malcolm, *Hotel Majestic*

1765

20 August

The issue of the *York Courant* for this day includes the earliest known reference to Harrogate's White Hart Hotel with this notice: '… Stray'd or convey'd on 14th August from Thomas Wray's at the White Hart in Low Harrogate, a dappled grey mare … whoever shall give notice of the same … 15 shillings reward and reasonable charges.' Precise origins are unknown, but it seems highly likely that the White Hart was first opened to cater for visitors to the nearby sulphur well or the cold well on Cold Bath Road.

The establishment of 200 acres of grassland or 'stray' on the inn's south side in 1778 provided an attractive, open approach to the building, which became an important venue for property auctions and a stopping point for coaches on major routes. Greater interest in the new science of hydrotherapy and the development of a railway network during the mid-nineteenth century brought increasing numbers of visitors to Harrogate and in 1847 a fine neoclassical-style building was completed on the original site. The hotel's popularity continued into the twentieth century with increasing trade as a conference centre, before it was requisitioned by the Air Ministry and Ministry of Works during the Second World War. In 1949, the White Hart became a conference centre for the National Health Service and in 1988 ownership passed to the University of York, before recent years brought a return to operations as a high-quality hotel and conference centre.

whitehart.net

1767

3 September

On this day, a perambulation involving commissioners and local people set out from Ribston with the purpose of defining and marking the boundaries of the Forest of Knaresborough. This area of ground covered about 40 square miles and contained twenty-four settlements between the rivers Nidd and Wharfe. Attempts to enclose the forest during the sixteenth and seventeenth centuries had failed in the face of local opposition, and matters were brought to a head by a large number of illegal encroachments.

An investigation in 1766 saw a Commission set up. Their initial task was to determine the forest boundaries. Following the perambulation, the boundary was marked by a series of forty-nine round-topped stones inscribed with the letters K-F and the date (usually 1767). The Commission also concluded that a considerable amount of the forest common was 'capable of cultivation and improvement', and this resulted in the Enclosure Act of 1770.

yorkshire-milestones.co.uk

1805

4 July

It was decided at a meeting on this day that a workhouse should be erected in the Harrogate area, and a plot of ground opposite the World's End Inn was identified as a suitable site. However, it was not until a further meeting on 1 June 1809 that a specially selected committee agreed to 'the expediency of opening or erecting a workhouse in order to reduce the poor rates and render the aged poor more comfortable.' Members of the committee appointed to organise the building of the workhouse included the tenants of the Crown, Dragon and Granby hotels (Joseph Thackwray, Joseph Goodlad and John Greeves respectively) along with one of Harrogate's leading physicians, Dr Jacques.

The selected site was at Starbeck and committee members identified 12 May 1810 as the completion date for building work. They also stipulated that their inspectors should monitor progress and arrange payment for the various stages of construction when they were satisfied with the standard of workmanship. It seems that the workhouse was completed by 12 May 1810.

Neesam, Malcolm, *Harrogate Great Chronicle 1332–1841*

1807

14 July

A newspaper article on this day stated:

Mrs. Addison respectfully informs her friends, her school (Grove House) re-opens the 27th inst., when she flatters herself, by every attention on her part, and that of approved masters, to merit the patronage of those who place their young ladies under her care. NB. Temporary boarders received during the season.

Grove House, located on Skipton Road, was built in the early 1750s as World's End Inn and claims to be the first house in Yorkshire to install gas lighting and heating. In 1805 it became a boarding school until 1809; brief periods of ownership then followed until the house was bought in 1850 by the engineering inventor, Samson Fox. Through his inventions, such as the corrugated flue, he amassed a considerable fortune which enabled him to complete the Royal Stables and a fully equipped workshop in the basement of Grove House. It was here that he produced water gas to provide lighting and heating for the building before extending the project into Harrogate. He also set up the town's first fire service and served as mayor for three successive years. Following his death in 1903, the house and grounds were maintained by staff. During the First World War, Grove House served as a convalescent hospital and between 1927 and 1947 it was an orphanage. In recent years, the premises have operated as a convalescent home and holiday centre.

west_cornwall_raob.tripod.com

1814

5 November

According to the records of Thomas Linforth, Overseer of the Poor in Harrogate, Widow Wetherill was given a pair of stockings, costing 2*s*, on this day. Other members of this family also suffered extreme hardship at about the same time. Thomas Wetherill's children contracted smallpox and when one of them died, the overseer paid 9*s* to cover the costs of the funeral. He also supplied a penny for thread to make shirts for John Wetherill, and William Wetherill's wife received three yards of flannel, which could be fashioned into a long winter petticoat. At this time, Widow Hardacre was supplied with two shifts by the overseer (these were short, straight garments, worn under a petticoat in the days before vests had been invented). Another needy lady, Dinah Leaf, received material to make two caps for night-time wear, while the overseer's detailed accounts indicated that Ann Waddington's son, Christopher, was awarded a coat, hat and breeches which cost 1*s* 6*d*, as well as thread to sew a couple of shirts.

Bebb, Prudence, *Life in Regency Harrogate*

1825

7 August

On this day, the foundation stone of St Mary's church was laid and building work in the Early English style was completed to designs by Mr Samuel Chapman of Leeds. During the 1860s, alterations were made in the form of the addition of a chancel (1865), replacement seating throughout the whole building in 1868 with the cost met by Miss Smith of the Belvedere, installation of a stained-glass window in 1862 as a memorial to the late Prince Albert (who had died in December the previous year) and a peal of six bells installed in the tower in 1866 with about £450 met by public subscriptions.

St Mary's had been built to provide Low Harrogate with a suitable match to the chapel of St John at High Harrogate. After a petition to the Duchy of Lancaster had gained approval in 1821, building work was subsequently completed at a cost of £3,137, making St Mary's the most expensive church building in Harrogate up to that date.

In 1904 the church was declared unsafe and it was eventually dismantled in 1923. The present church of St Mary was completed as a replacement in 1916 to designs in a fourteenth-century style by Walter Tapper.

Grainge, William, *History and Topology of Harrogate*

1835

1 December

On the morning of this day, the proprietor of the Swan Inn, Jonathan Shutt, left his premises to walk along Swan Road towards the Old Sulphur Well. As he passed a shop owned by Joseph Thackwray, part of the adjacent Crown Hotel building, Shutt noticed unexpected activity inside the building. Closer inspection revealed that workmen were excavating a deep well which was within 20 yards of two of the three existing sulphur wells at Low Harrogate, and Shutt immediately alerted leading citizens about his concerns. The prevailing opinion was that Joseph Thackwray was attempting to divert the waters of the public sulphur well into his own property so that he could achieve a monopoly.

Meetings took place in the town's Promenade Rooms and, following Thackwray's refusal to halt his digging, a group of senior citizens agreed to prosecute him. A protracted case was finally resolved at York Assizes when Joseph Thackwray was acquitted on a technicality, but increased public support saw the Harrogate Improvement Bill become law. During 1841 the town elected twenty-one 'improvement commissioners' to govern and oversee improvements by making use of a limited power to rate.

Walker, Harold Hyde, *History of Harrogate*

1837

10 August

A poster displaying this date advertised goods for sale at the Oriental Lounge, High Harrogate, owned by Antonio Fattorini:

> … [The owner] respectfully announces to the visitors and inhabitants of Harrogate, that he has on hand a large stock of jewellery, Sheffield Plated Goods and Berlin Silver, which he is enabled to offer at extremely low prices. Also Ladies and Gentlemen's Dressing Cases, Writing Desk, Work Boxes, Umbrellas, Parasols and a variety of other articles. Cut Glass Decanters, Tumblers and a variety of table lamps etc.

Antonio Fattorini was born in Italy in 1797 and moved to England during unrest created by the Napoleonic Wars. In 1831 he and his wife moved to Harrogate and opened their Oriental Lounge at 14 Regent Parade to serve wealthy visitors during the town's exclusive summer season. Antonio died in 1859 and his son, Antonio Jr, continued the business and moved to No.2 Crown Place during the mid-1870s. When Harrogate became a borough in 1884, Fattorini's provided the mayoral chain. A further move saw the company based in their present property at No.10 Parliament Street, where the business is now operated by descendants of Antonio Fattorini, the Tindall family.

Neesam, Malcolm, *Images of England: Harrogate*

1843

4 January

On this day Charles Greeves, a local land surveyor, noted in his diary that he had completed the 'Stray gates plan of roads and the slips on the sides'. He had been commissioned to compile the survey in the autumn of the previous year and his findings stated that the Stray contained 201 acres and 3.91 roods, and the slips totalled 19 acres 2.22 roods, which amounted to an overall total of 221 acres and 2.13 roods. (One rood equates to a quarter of an acre.) Payment for his professional services for the survey amounted to £11 13s 0d. Previously, Greeves had been actively involved with the Stray Committee by checking on encroachments; his efforts prevented the multiplication of Stray Gates – at that time a common method of gaining money for improvements.

Walker, Harold Hyde, *History of Harrogate*

1843

11 July

Thomas Thrush – 'the warrior turned Christian' – died at Bellevue in Harrogate on this day, just short of his 82nd birthday. Born in Stockton-on-Tees in July 1761, his family moved to Richmond when he was young and he was educated at the town's grammar school before studying the French language in York. Returning to Richmond, he completed an apprenticeship as a draper in 1782, but then took up a career at sea with a post on a merchant ship. His personal and naval qualities saw Thrush earn promotion in the Royal Navy during the early 1800s; during the late months of 1806 he was sent to the West Indies in command of the *Avon*. In July 1809 he gained a commission as a post captain and was given command of a frigate for the remaining years of the war against France. Thomas Thrush seemed to be destined to achieve the rank of admiral, but on 14 January 1825 he resigned his commission and wrote to the king, George IV (pictured opposite), outlining his reasons for this action. His convictions as a Christian had led to this momentous decision, which was explained in his work *Observations on the causes and evils of war; its unlawfulness and the means and certainty of its extinction.*

jstor.org

1843

22 August

The death of Mrs Elizabeth Lupton was reported on this day. Aged 83, she was well known locally as 'Old Betty, Queen of the Wells', and had served sulphur water for more than sixty years. Women had dispensed water at the wells for over a century, but it seems that this work took a toll. According to Thomas Baskerville, '… their faces did shine like bacon rind. And for beauty many vie with an old Bath guide's ass, the sulphur waters had so fouled their pristine complexions.'

Elizabeth Lupton, popularly known as Betty Lupton, was described as 'a privileged person' who 'dispenses the waters and quodlibets [a humorous medley of tunes] with equal liberality'. Contemporary illustrations depict her dressed in an apron and bonnet, carrying a long-handled water dispenser and glass tumbler. The Queen of the Wells was elected annually from the town's volunteer water servers, with a coronation held each May. On her retirement, Old Betty was rewarded with an allowance of 1s a day from the Harrogate Improvement Commissioners, who had built the Royal Pump Room over the Old Sulphur Well.

northyorksgov.uk

1845

7 July

Dr George Kennion (1813–1868) was first appointed as a Harrogate Commissioner on this date. His last appearance as a member of the Board of Commissioners was at a meeting on 2 January 1863, and it is generally acknowledged that he was the finest of all the board members. During the late 1840s, many of the commissioners' meetings were characterised by endless squabbles and irrelevant litigation, most notably when gas lighting was installed in Harrogate during 1847. Arguments between commissioners and the gas company lasted for months, and in a letter to the *Harrogate Advertiser* dated 16 May 1849, Dr Kennion warned local folk about the situation:

… Unless the inhabitants of Harrogate – whether of High Harrogate or Low Harrogate – whether Commissioners or non-commissioners – unless all unite together, and throwing aside past differences and all littleness of mere party feeling – join together in furthering the real interests of Harrogate … this place, which is so favoured by nature, and which has so much in itself to attract the invalid as well as the visitor who merely seeks for recreation, will gradually fall from being the most important watering place of the north to the position of the most insignificant of Spas … I have heard remarks such as the following: 'Harrogate: Who would go there that could help it? Nothing is done to make the place comfortable. The people are all too busy quarrelling among themselves to have any time or attention to throw away upon visitors.'

1847

6 December

A meeting of the town's commissioners on this day considered the question of an agreement with a company for the supply of lamps that provided street lighting. Further discussion concluded a 'scale' of lamp lighting, which defined times when the lamps should burn, would be suitable: The lamps were to be lit from 1 November to 1 May between sunset and 1 a.m. During the following three months, there would be no street lighting, before lights were again lit during August, September and October from sunset to 3 a.m. At this same meeting it was agreed to levy a rate of 3*d* in the pound, to be collected before 5 April 1848. Ten of the fifteen commissioners voted in favour, with one against. Further business focused on the question of an agreement with the company and, after protracted discussions, a sum of £2 5*s* per lamp was finalised for nine months of the following year.

The complexity and protracted nature of discussions over the provision of gas street lighting at this meeting typify the difficulties posed by this matter for Harrogate Commissioners from the mid-1840s.

Walker, Harold Hyde, *History of Harrogate*

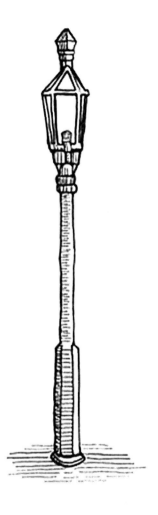

1850

3 July

On this day, a train pulling fifty-four carriages arrived at Harrogate's Brunswick station. More than 2,000 visitors from the Sheffield area stepped on to the platform for a day trip to the popular spa town. The *Harrogate Advertiser* reported that 'the road down West Park and Parliament Street presented one moving mass of human beings, wending their way towards the Cheltenham Spa Rooms, where a great number partook of tea in the afternoon.' Such a spectacle was so rare that many local people made their way to the station at 6.30 p.m. to watch the train depart.

Brunswick railway station had been opened on 20 July 1848, after considerable opposition from the local population who feared not only the noise, smoke and smells that would result, but also the arrival of less affluent, common people who would take advantage of this cheap form of transport. The new station was a very short distance from the Tewit Well, which fortunately was not affected by excavation work. If damage had been done to the well, the Harrogate Commissioners made it clear that they would demand another replacement well be located and equipped.

Mitchell, W.R., *Harrogate Past*

1855

5 November

On this day, Richard Ellis reported to the Improvement Commissioners for Harrogate that prices for fire engines had been obtained, and after discussing the subject, the commissioners decided to spend no more than £120 on such a piece of equipment. By 1858, the existence of a fire engine in the town seemed to have been forgotten and in 1861, reports indicated that it was in a state of disrepair. Two years later, Ellis asked for an update on the situation, only to be told that it had been lost; further (intermittent) enquiries proved fruitless. Eventually, in 1872, it was established that the engine and pump had been removed for alternative use and during the following year the commissioners were given assurances that the engine had been reassembled and was in full working order. Unfortunately there was no horse to draw the engine and when one was located, the animal only had sight in one eye. However, by 1874, these setbacks had apparently been overcome. James Lomas declared that it was safe and in full working order, only for its severe limitations to be exposed when dealing with a fire at the Swan Hydro in October 1878. Fortunately, there were few fires of a serious nature during this period of deficiency in terms of a fire service.

Walker, Harold Hyde, *History of Harrogate*

1861

12 January

A report in the *Leeds Mercury* on this day described the difficulties faced by many local families because of a spell of 'protracted frost' in the Harrogate area. Particularly badly affected were dependants of menfolk based at the railway works, where the cold spell had brought a suspension of work. During the previous week, a fund had been set up to arrange for 'relief of the destitute', and already nearly 400 families had been given assistance. Relief provided consisted of soup, coal, bread and flour 'amounting to £58', and with subscriptions totalling more than £130, an 'active committee' still had a fund of £70 to administer. A meeting of the Relief Committee reached the decision to offer employment to navvies who had been laid off at the railway works. They would be offered work such as cleaning footpaths in the neighbourhood and, the *Leeds Mercury* reported, this would hopefully end the practice of begging, which was 'rapidly becoming a nuisance in this place'.

1862

1 August

This day saw the closure of Brunswick railway station, which was located on Trinity Road beside The Stray, after just fourteen years of operational service. (Powers had been obtained in the North Eastern Railways Act to bring all Harrogate's services in to one centrally sited station.) One enduring feature of the early route on the approach to Brunswick station is a 400-yard long tunnel that remains in remarkably good condition, albeit with imprints along the floor caused by railway sleepers.

During the Second World War the tunnel was adopted as an air-raid shelter, with a flight of steps giving access to it from the area of the Leeds Road roundabout. Within the tunnel, 6ft-high blast walls were constructed, and wooden benches fitted along both sides. Toilet cubicles were located in all four corners and electric cabling provided light and power during the war years.

The air-raid shelter was abandoned in 1943 and remained largely forgotten, as shown in the 1960s when workmen constructing the roundabout inadvertently dug into the roof level. (The tunnel entrance is on private land and not open to the public.)

BBC News

1865

17 August

On this day, the foundation stone was laid for Victoria Park Methodist church. The architect was J.H. Hirst of Bristol, and he created a distinctive and unconventional Victorian Gothic style. When the church was opened for worship on 17 August 1865, building costs had risen from an initial estimate of £3,400 to £4,995 9s 10d, but outstanding debts on the church and nearby Sunday school were cleared by Richard Ellis, who had already provided land for building work. He also arranged for Richmond Villa in Raglan Street to become the manse for the Methodist minister.

As a staunch Methodist, Richard Ellis had played a leading role in establishing the movement in Harrogate, initially with his support for Salem chapel in James Street. Construction of Victoria Park Methodist church was part of the overall development at this location, which was intended to include a town hall at the corner of Victoria Avenue.

After standing empty during the immediate post-war years, the church building was taken over by the Cooperative Society and demolished in the early months of 1954. Co-op premises were later constructed on the site.

Neesam, Malcolm, *Bygone Harrogate*

1866

5 March

The monthly meeting of the Harrogate Improvement Commissioners was held on this day, with eleven commissioners attending and Richard Ellis as chairman. Business discussed included the question of parliamentary representation of Harrogate, and Edward Pullan outlined the need to have Harrogate included within the Knaresborough Electoral District. It was agreed that the increase in population and wealth of Harrogate warranted parliamentary representation, and that a committee should be set up to forward a statement to the government for inclusion of the Improvement District of Harrogate with the Borough of Knaresborough under terms of the forthcoming Reform Bill.

Committee members forwarded the statement to Lord Frederick Cavendish, MP for Knaresborough, with the request that he submit it to Parliament. Progress appears to have been predictably slow, but Lord Cavendish did receive an acknowledgement dated 19 March 1866:

> My Lord,
>
> I am directed by Secretary Sir George Grey to acknowledge the receipt of your letter of the 16th Instant, forwarding a Memorial of the Improvement Commissioners of High and Low Harrogate, praying that in any measure for the redistribution of seats in the House of Commons the claims of the Harrogate Improvement District to be limited to the Borough of Knaresborough may be considered. I have the honour to be, My Lord, Your Lordship's obedient servant, J. Baring.

Walker, Harold Hyde, *History of Harrogate*

1866

23 June

On this day a group of workmen were quarrying limestone in the area known as the Bogs when they uncovered an old level or drift tunnel. Measuring between 4 and 5ft in height and about 3ft 6in in width, it had been roughly carved through the rock towards the rear of Binns' Hotel. The workmen followed the tunnel for a short distance and came across several pieces of candle, which had evidently been left by miners during excavation of the driftway. The workmen concluded that the tunnel had resulted from a fruitless search for lead ore.

Close examination of the material did reveal the presence of small fragments of shiny stone which were sufficiently hard to scratch glass. These were known locally as 'Harrogate diamonds' and it was widely reported that when topsoil in the locality was disturbed during ploughing or by heavy rainfall, these 'diamonds' could be found twinkling like little stars among the soil.

Grainge, William, *The History and Topology of Harrogate*

1870

25 August

On this day a lifeboat arrived in Harrogate, and it was positioned in the grounds of the Royal Chalybeate Spa under the supervision of Captain Ward, Inspector of Lifeboats to the Royal National Lifeboat Institution. The cost of the lifeboat had been met by the Misses Carter, who lived at Vine Villa, James Street, Harrogate and more than 700 members of the public came to view the vessel, which measured 33ft in length by 8½ft wide with ten oars double banked.

Two days later a procession took place. Crew members dressed in appropriate costume and holding their oars in an upright position accompanied the lifeboat as it travelled through the town's central streets. It was appropriately named *The Sisters Carter of Harrogate*.

This tradition of supporting lifeboat charities continued into the twentieth century with celebrations on 23 July 1904 in aid of the Hartlepool Lifeboat Fund. A procession led by the Borough Band started from the Victoria Baths in Crescent Gardens with a variety of floats making their way around the town before gathering on the town's football ground.

Neesam, Malcolm, *Images of England: Harrogate*

1871

26 August

The New Victoria Baths in Crescent Garden were opened on this day with a gala in the Spa Rooms. Plans for the building had been drawn up by the town's surveyor, James Richardson, who utilised designs put forward by various other architects, and rooms above the central entrance hall were used by the Harrogate Improvement Commissioners. Though this setting has seen endless debates, fewer occasions can have been more tense than the gathering on 9 May 1900, when an inquiry was held by the local government board to investigate Harrogate Corporation's borrowing the huge sum of £35,000 to finance the waterworks scheme.

In 1931, the Victoria Baths were reconstructed by Leonard Clarke; the municipal buildings and rooms above the central entrance, previously used by the Improvement Commissioners, became the council chamber. When a road was constructed in front of the buildings, a decision was taken to retain a mature evergreen tree in the middle of the highway, presumably as a measure to restrict traffic speed.

Neesam, Malcolm, *Bygone Harrogate*

1874

28 February

On this day John Barber, Commissioners' chairman for the year 1873–74, laid the foundation stone of Harrogate's first market building on land adjacent to Cambridge Street and Beulah Terrace (later Station Square). The need for a market in the town had been raised in the 1840s, often with backing in the columns of the *Harrogate Advertiser*, but it was only in November 1865 that the commissioners began serious discussion on the matter. Finally, on 22 December 1873, they approved plans by Arthur Hiscoe which included a clock tower at the corner of Beulah Terrace and Cambridge Street and a weigh house at the rear of the premises. It was appropriate that John Barber should lay the foundation stone, as he had consistently advocated the need for a market.

Building work proceeded rapidly and the market was opened on 29 August 1874, exactly six months since the foundation stone had been laid. A procession from the commissioners' headquarters at the Victoria Baths was led by the Harrogate Rifle Volunteers and on reaching the market hall there were speeches by Henry Greensmith, chairman of the Commissioners and George Dawson, chairman of the Market Committee.

Walker, Harold Hyde, *History of Harrogate*

1877

9 June

Harrogate Cricket Club was formed at a meeting in the town's Somerset Hotel on this day. Land adjacent to St George's Road was leased at an annual rent of £24 and the first match took place on 7 July 1877. Apart from club matches, an England XI, including W.G. Grace, played an Australian touring side in September 1885 and between 1880 and 1902 several England games were staged on the St George's Road pitch. In 1890, women's cricket was played at the Harrogate ground for the first time. Reports in the *Harrogate Advertiser* stated that: '… their skirts are long and the edge is weighted down with lead shots so that they did not lift in the wind.' Four years later the first Yorkshire County match took place and this was followed by the opening of a pavilion in August 1896, at a cost of £900.

During the early 1930s, foreign touring sides played at Harrogate – New Zealand in 1931, India in 1932 and the West Indies a year later, but difficult financial times left the club close to bankruptcy. The 'situation' was relieved when the town council purchased the land, paid off the club's debts and arranged for Harrogate Cricket Club to become tenants. Cricket festivals became an annual feature at the ground during the twentieth century, and a highlight of the club's recent history was an appearance in the final of the National Knockout Cup at Lord's Cricket Ground in 1998.

pitchero.com

1878

5 August

On this day, the Bicycle Touring Club was founded at Harrogate's St George Inn after a Scotsman, Stanley John Ambrose Cotterell, is said to have pedalled his penny farthing or 'High Ordinary' bicycle all the way from Edinburgh to meet like-minded 'velocipede enthusiasts' from many parts of the United Kingdom. Initially the club had eighty members, all of them men, and in 1880 the first woman, Mrs W.D. Welford, was given membership. During the early years of the organisation, its headquarters depended on where Stanley Cotterell was living at the time.

In 1883 the Bicycle Touring Club was renamed the Cyclists' Touring Club, to allow membership for tricyclists and a headquarters was set up at 139–140 Fleet Street, London. One of Cotterell's initial tasks was to organise a network of hotels for use by members, and by the early 1880s, contracts had been arranged with 785 venues. Members of the CTC could stay at these hotels for a fixed tariff with exclusive use of lounges.

On the 75th anniversary of Stanley Cotterell's ride from Edinburgh to Harrogate, the event was re-enacted and a commemorative plaque was unveiled.

ctc.org.uk

1879

25 February

One of Harrogate's most prominent citizens, Lieutenant Colonel John James Harrison, died at the age of 57 at his residence, Devonshire House in High Harrogate. With long-established links to North Yorkshire, the Harrison family moved to Ripon in the early eighteenth century and after travelling abroad for two years during his youth, John Harrison based himself in Harrogate in 1848. He was a senior partner in the Old Bank when it was taken over by the Bradford Old Banking Company and became managing director of the Harrogate section. In 1854, he became a magistrate and when he stood for election as one of the commissioners for the town, he narrowly failed to top the poll. An interest in field sports saw him become master of the Harrogate Harriers and he was instrumental in establishing a Rifle Volunteer Corps. Fellow members unanimously elected him as their first captain, and further promotion saw him become a major and then, in 1873, lieutenant colonel. Contemporary reports indicate that his ability to combine a genial personality with a strong will to achieve the highest standards brought John Harrison considerable respect and affection in mid-nineteenth-century Harrogate.

Harrogate Advertiser

1884

6 February

A Charter of Incorporation reached Harrogate by train on this day. Granted by Queen Victoria, it was delivered by Mr A. Malcolm Betson, solicitor to the commissioners, amid a dramatic burst of celebratory explosions from fog signals positioned along the track. Prominent local citizens lined the platform and a procession of carriages were drawn up outside in readiness to carry the charter through the streets to the New Victoria Baths, where a dais had been installed on the steps.

This development resulted in the election of a full council on a ward basis, the office of mayor and procedures which would facilitate appropriate improvements for the expanding community. Under the terms of the charter, Robert Ackrill was appointed as mayor and assessor for revising the burgess lists, while W. Henry Wyles was to serve as town clerk.

In celebration of the Incorporation of Harrogate, a grand banquet was held at the town's Crown Hotel on 12 February 1884 with about 100 guests and a Dr Myrtle presiding. After grace had been said, there was a toast to the queen and this was followed by a considerable number of speeches which grew in length as a series of additional toasts exerted influence.

Walker, Harold Hyde, *History of Harrogate*

1885

28 November

On this day Samson Fox, industrialist and benefactor to the townspeople of Harrogate, delivered a speech in St James' Hall, Cambridge Street, in which he outlined his support for the policy of protectionism. During the 1870s he devoted a considerable amount of time and energy developing his business interests; most notably in 1877, when he took out patents on his invention, the corrugated boiler flue. Five years later, further patents were issued for another of his inventions, the pressed steel railway bogie. With this background, he was well placed to speak out on matters relating to business and industry, but in addition the 1880s saw him develop closer links with Harrogate and the local population. In 1882, Samson Fox set up the Leeds Forge Band, which often gave performances at Grove House, his home in Harrogate, or at other venues in the town, and in 1886 he invited the renowned Croatian painter, Vlaho Bukovac, to visit Grove House. This led to him acquiring several fine artworks, one of which, *Jesus and the Children*, was later displayed in St Robert's church. Most memorable, though, for many local residents was the ox roasting in celebration of Queen Victoria's Golden Jubilee in 1887 when around 4,000 people gathered on High Harrogate Stray. Two years later, in July 1889, Fox paid for the completion of two ornamental arches over the route taken by Prince Albert Victor during a visit to open the Royal Bath Hospital.

Neesam, Malcolm, *Bygone Harrogate*

1887

20 June

An ox-roasting ceremony got underway on The Stray at High Harrogate to celebrate Queen Victoria's Golden Jubilee. The spit was turned for twenty-four hours as the ox was roasted and, with dusk approaching after a day of glorious sunshine, a band played. 'Soft beams' from Samson Fox's electric lighting system illuminated the scene as dancers performed waltzes, polkas and quadrilles across the level expanse of The Stray. At noon the following day portions of roast beef, bread and beer were distributed to a huge crowd and a joyous atmosphere was enlivened by performances from itinerant entertainers. Officers of the law were present in the form of Inspector Lamb and two constables but they were merely onlookers as the previous evening's programme of band music and dancing continued to a late hour on the second day. Contemporary reports describe Mr Samson Fox, who provided the ox, dressed in double-breasted reefer coat and flat-peaked cap as he supervised the roasting.

Neesam, Malcolm, *Exclusively Harrogate*

1887

6 October

On this day the Marquis of Ripon unveiled the Victoria Monument in celebration of the Queen's Golden Jubilee. Sited on land in front of the town's railway station, the monument – complete with Gothic-style canopy – was the work of local architects H.E. and A. Brown, while the statue itself was sculpted by a London craftsman named Webber. The cost of the monument was met by Harrogate's mayor, Alderman Richard Ellis. He and his wife also laid the foundation stone on 23 June 1887.

When it was first installed, the monument was surrounded by decorative cast-iron railings and gas lamps but these were removed during the Second World War. Its location at the entrance to James Street meant that the statue of the queen would be passed by visitors arriving by carriage in the town. The unveiling of the monument was one of the several events held in Harrogate to celebrate the queen's Golden Jubilee and these included an ox roasting for the people of the town on The Stray.

Smith, Roly, *Harrogate: A History and Celebration*

1888

8 June

On this day the decision was made to form a free subscription band in Harrogate. Residents of the town agreed to subscribe funds for the formation of a permanent brass band with J. Sidney Jones, bandmaster of the Leeds Rifles, as its conductor. Some five weeks later, on 16 July 1888, the band performed its first concert in Montpellier Gardens under his leadership.

The bandmaster's responsibilities were considerable as his bandsmen met a demanding schedule. A daily performance took place at 7.30 a.m. for visitors who needed to 'take the waters', and there were three further concerts during the morning and early afternoon in support of the gentle recreations that formed part of the 'cure'. Bandsmen were required to appear in top hats at each of their four daily performances for a wage of no more than £1 per week. Much of the band's continuing success must be credited to J. Sidney Jones, who qualified as a bandmaster while serving in the Dragoon Guards. After moving to Yorkshire, he coached brass bands before moving from Leeds Rifles to Harrogate.

harrogateband.org

1890

3 June

At exactly 3 p.m. on this day, one of Harrogate's most imposing properties, The Cairn, came under the auctioneer's hammer at the salerooms of Messrs Hirst and Capes. Advertising literature described it as '… the estate known as The Cairn, situated on the summit of Ripon Road, along with gardens, tennis courts, stables and a coach house'. The vendor was its current owner, A.E. Harter Esq. He had constructed 'The Cairn' for his own use and was reported to be extremely sad about the sale of the property, which was leasehold from the Duchy of Lancaster for an annual rental charge of £62.

Just sixteen months after the sale, however, disaster struck when the entire east wing was destroyed in a fire that began when a servant ignited a curtain with a lighted candle. Major refurbishment soon took place and an extension was completed, with the result that 'The Cairn' became widely known as a 'desirable gentleman's hunting lodge'. In 1898, the charges were £3 17s 0d or £5 5s 0d per person per week depending on the quality of room, and this included an attendant, morning bath, breakfast, lunch, afternoon tea and dinner. Fires in the bedrooms cost either 2s per day, 1s 6d for the afternoon or just 1s for the evening only.

strathmorehotels.com

1890

24 July

Charles Hull was born in Harrogate on this day and worked as a postman before joining the 21st Lancers (Empress of India's) in the British Army. He was serving as a private on the North-West Frontier of India when his actions on 5 September 1915 resulted in him being awarded the Victoria Cross.

The citation, published in the *London Gazette* on 3 March 1916, stated:

> 1053 Private (Shoeing Smith) Charles Hull, 21st Lancers. For most conspicuous bravery. When under close fire of the enemy, who were within a few yards, he rescued Captain G.E.D. Learoyd, whose horse had been shot, by taking him up behind him and galloping into safety. Shoeing-Smith Hull acted entirely on his own initiative, and saved his officer's life at the imminent risk of his own.

He was later promoted to the rank of corporal and during the 1920s, Charles Hull served as a police officer with the Leeds Constabulary. He died in Leeds on 21 February 1953.

Wikipedia

1890

3 December

Donald Simpson Bell was born in Harrogate on this day. He was educated at Harrogate Grammar School before furthering his studies at Westminster College. Bell also excelled at sport and played as an amateur with Crystal Palace and then Newcastle before returning to his birthplace as a teacher at Starbeck School. During 1912, he signed professional forms as a footballer with Bradford Park Avenue and made his debut during the following season.

When war broke out, Bell joined the West Yorkshire Regiment; he is widely regarded as the first professional footballer to enlist in the British Army. Rapid promotion saw Donald Bell become an officer in the 9th Battalion of the Yorkshire Regiment (the 'Green Howards') in 1915 and on the evening of 5 July 1916, his actions during an attack on a German position at Horseshoe Trench during the Battle of the Somme near La Boiselle earned him the Victoria Cross.

Just five days later, and unaware of his award, Donald Bell was fatally injured during an attack on another German position at Contalmaison. His widow received the Victoria Cross from King George V in a private ceremony at Buckingham Palace on 13 December 1916, and in July 2000 a memorial was unveiled at the place where he died, with an inscription dedicated to 'the First English Professional Footballer to enlist in 1914 and the only Professional Footballer to be awarded the Victoria Cross'. His medal was eventually sold at the Spink saleroom, in London, on 25 November 2010 for £210,000.

BBC News

1892

4 March

A meeting was held at the Queen Hotel overlooking The Stray at Harrogate, with the aim of forming a golf club somewhere in the town. Little more than three months later, a course was opened on land beside Irongate Bridge Road and on 10 June 1892, *Golf* magazine reported:

> … The course is situated about a quarter of an hour's walk from the Pump Room and is conveniently placed for those who are taking the waters. It is in the direction of Birk Crag. Part of the links is about 500 feet above sea level and is swept by invigorating breezes from the Yorkshire Wolds. As regards picturesque surroundings it is second to none in the kingdom …

A pavilion was erected at a cost of £125 and although no refreshments were provided, teas were available from a Miss White, who lived in the cottage opposite. The club's first professional player was Tom Chisholm of St Andrews, who was paid 22*s* per week. The annual subscription fee was £1 1*s* 0*d*.

Problems arose, however, when the club's landlord, the Duchy of Lancaster, approved construction of a slaughterhouse close to the pavilion during 1895. In February 1898 the committee signed a lease to develop a course at Belmont Farm.

Golf magazine

1892

15 September

On this day, Heatherdene Convalescent Home was opened on land beside Wetherby Road in a ceremony performed by Mrs Stansfield Richardson, Mayoress of Sunderland. Funds for this facility had been raised following a tragedy at the Victoria Hall in Sunderland, when 183 children were suffocated or crushed to death during a stampede.

When subscription funds were exhausted, Heatherdene was operated by Sunderland Royal Infirmary, and many miners from the North-East were sent there for convalescence. A new wing was added in 1894 and during the First World War, the premises housed a hospital for wounded servicemen under the management of the Grand Duchess George of Russia. In 1918 she was joined as matron by Miss Mary Macrea, who served there until her death in 1931. She was succeeded by Miss H. Dodd.

With the establishment of the National Health Service, Heatherdene was brought into use as a convalescent home for women and it continued in this role until the 1960s.

Neesam, Malcolm, *Bygone Harrogate*

1895

21 August

Richard Ellis, a major figure in the development of Victorian Harrogate, died on this day. Elected as an Improvement Commissioner in 1855, he worked tirelessly to bring about schemes that would benefit the town, including the adoption of the Local Government Act in 1858. In addition to serving as magistrate, he was Mayor of Harrogate between 1884 and 1887. General benefits for townspeople resulted from his involvement in the foundation of Ashville School, along with his support for a cottage hospital and for an effective sewage system in the town. When plans were made to link railway lines from Leeds and Knaresborough, he was instrumental in ensuring that the new line ran through a cutting and that loss of land on The Stray was replaced by adding the site of the old Brunswick station. Initially, access to the station was only possible from the west side, so in 1875, Richard Ellis built a new road, East Parade.

Ellis' last major scheme was for the establishment of an international standard bathing and hydrotherapy centre. Following his death, the project was successfully completed in 1897 at a cost of £120,000, with support from the town's mayor, Charles Fortune.

Mitchell, W.R., *Harrogate Past*

1897

23 July

Harrogate Royal Baths were officially opened on this day by HRH Prince George, the Duke of Cambridge. The scheme for a bathing and hydrotherapy centre of international status had been promoted by Richard Ellis, and building work was carried out by Baggalley and Bristowe of London at a cost of £120,000. An overall Moorish design featured spreading Islamic arches and screens, walls of vibrant glazed brickwork, arabesque painted ceilings and terrazzo floors, laid by specialist Italian craftsmen. Water was pumped directly to the baths from several local springs and a peat bath was available, while seawater – for a brine bath – was transported by rail from Teesside. In total there was a choice of almost forty different kinds of bath for visitors, and treatments were available for people suffering from gout, rheumatism, arthritis, sciatica, lumbago, skin diseases and liver and kidney conditions. With some justification, it was claimed that Harrogate's Royal Baths represented the most advanced centre for hydrotherapy anywhere in the world.

W.R. Mitchell, *Harrogate Past*

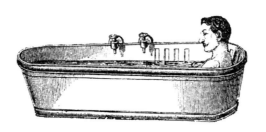

1900

13 January

Harrogate Theatre opened its doors to the public for the first time on this day. At that time it was known as the 'Harrogate Grand Opera House' and the initial show, attended by the town's mayoress, Mrs James Myrtle, was a charity performance of *Gentlemen in Khaki* to support troops involved in the Boer War.

The architect was Frank Tugwell, who also designed the Futurist Theatre at Scarborough and London's Savoy Theatre. A feature of his work at Harrogate was an unusual art nouveau frieze in the entrance hall. A suspended canopy that offered shelter to pedestrians on the front street was removed after the First World War.

During January 1933 Harrogate Theatre became the base for the White Rose Players, one of the first permanent repertory companies in this country. They staged about forty-five shows each year, with weekly changes of bill, and notable members included Trevor Howard, who worked there in the 1930s, and Brian Rix, who made appearances in the following decade. One of the original White Rose Players, Valerie Woodings, was invited to unveil a heritage plaque in celebration of the theatre's 110th birthday.

'Harrogate Theatre celebrates its 110th anniversary', BBC News

1900

18 July

The formal opening of Harrogate's Hotel Majestic took place, with welcome speeches from the management followed by a reception for 600 people, followed by a banquet for 130 honoured guests. A tour of inspection began in the hotel's great lounge, where guests admired the splendid marble cladding, staircase and murals of English spa resorts before moving on through public rooms, which included the drawing room, dining room and billiard rooms, the latter having an enormous chimney piece. Led by Sir Blundell Maple, the group then entered the winter garden – all 8,000ft^2 of it – and he proudly explained that the planting of the central area was in single containers. This arrangement allowed flexibility within the glazed interior to create space for events such as a banquet. In his concluding remarks at the end of the tour, Sir Blundell Maple drew attention to other facilities within the hotel – including the ladies and gentlemen's hairdressing departments in the basement – before the group returned to the dining hall.

Neesam, Malcolm, *Hotel Majestic*

1900

20 July

Maurice Leyland, one of Yorkshire and England's finest cricketers, was born on this day in Harrogate. A natural left-handed batsman and bowler, he learned much about cricket from his father and by the age of 14, he was playing in Lancashire League cricket. After serving in the army during the First World War, Maurice Leyland played professionally for the Harrogate club between 1918 and 1920 before playing his first match for Yorkshire, against Essex, in 1920. Over the next twenty-nine years, he scored 33,660 runs in first-class cricket at an average of 40.50, and 26,191 for his county side, at an average of 41.05.

Leyland won his county cap in 1922, and during the following season he reached 1,000 runs for the first time – a feat that he achieved every season until the outbreak of the Second World War in 1939. His Test debut for England came during the 1928–29 tour of Australia and over the next ten seasons he became renowned for impeccable defence, along with supreme determination when retrieving his team's fortunes. Though his bowling skills were rarely called for, Maurice Leyland was a fine left-arm bowler and he also showed great prowess in almost any fielding position. Between 1951 and 1963, he was a coach at Yorkshire C.C. but following a long illness, he died at hospital in Harrogate on 1 January 1967.

espncricinfo.com

1901

15 April

On this day, Harrogate Council completed the purchase of Collins Field, with the intention of adding it to the Valley Gardens. For the next ten years, however, a solid stone wall blocked access from the gardens to the Bog Fields and it was Councillor Binns, chairman of the Valley Gardens Committee, along with a group of workmen, who demolished it at dead of night on 13 February 1911.

Work could now proceed on a lime walk through the middle of the site; a series of paths were laid out, trees were planted and ornamental borders created. A rustic tea house with veranda was constructed on the slopes of the former Collins Field overlooking a bandstand, located close to the new Magnesia Well pump room.

In 1912, a new entrance was created opposite the pump room, complete with ornamental gates and railings. During the 1920s, recreational facilities were added, in the form of golf greens and tennis courts. A highlight of the interwar era for the Valley Gardens was the staging of the first horticultural show in September 1934.

The post-war years have seen further development of the Valley Gardens, including a New Zealand Garden stocked with plants, supplied on an exchange basis, from that country as well as the inclusion of additional recreational areas. The 1980s also saw the establishment of the Friends of Valley Gardens, following the removal of horticultural shows and the demise of the Sun Pavilion.

friendsofvalleygardens.co.uk

1902

1 January

This day saw the laying of the foundation stone of the Kursaal by Alderman Simpson, following protracted deliberations about the scheme in council meetings. During the early months of 1899, a design competition was held and on 1 August in the same year, a report was received from Frank Matcham, who had been formally appointed assessor in the previous year. The successful scheme was submitted by Robert J. Beale, and Matcham became consulting architect.

Beale's original plans included a 3,000-seat concert hall, a smoking room, a reading room, a French restaurant and café as well as an external porte-cochère for carriages but the council ruled an estimated cost of £50,000 to be prohibitive. A revised scheme reduced the cost to around £35,000, and the scheme soon got underway. Considering the amount of time taken up during the planning stages, construction work was completed surprisingly quickly and Sir Hubert Parry performed the official opening on 28 May 1903.

The outbreak of war in 1914 precipitated a wave of anti-German emotion and in February 1915 it was decided that the 'Kursaal' should be renamed 'The Coliseum'. Official approval for this change was delayed, but during the interwar years it became 'The Royal Hall' – although the original name remains prominently displayed on the stone façade.

Quin, Stuart, *Kursaal: A History of Harrogate's Royal Hall*

1902

24 August

Initial plans for an Anglo-Catholic place of worship on Harrogate's Duchy estate resulted in the first congregation assembling on this day in a corrugated-iron building on an empty plot of ground adjacent to Duchy Road. Early fundraising efforts seemed to point towards a church of modest proportions, but the generosity of Miss Elizabeth Sophia Trotter, which included a contribution of £10,000 and a legacy of £32,000, led to the commissioning of Temple Lushington Moore as architect and plans for a larger church. Building work on St Wilfrid's was unfinished when Temple Moore suffered a brain haemorrhage on 30 June 1920 and died soon afterwards, but the project was completed by his son-in-law, Leslie Moore.

The addition of a lady chapel in 1935 augmented the overall setting, which embodies space and light. Mainly thirteenth century in style, it has a clerestoried nave with aisles, a chancel with triforium and clerestory and chapels as well as a low embattled tower with a pyramid roof over the crossing. Most of the glass in the church is the work of Victor Milner, and it is his judicious use of plain glass that provides a brighter interior. Items such as the Arts and Crafts-style lectern, the processional cross and sanctuary lamp were gifts to the church while a set of Stations of the Cross were donated in memory of Vernon Taylor by his family members.

St Wilfrid's Church, Harrogate guidebook

1903

9 February

William Best died on this day at Grangeville, Walker Road in Harrogate at the age of 73. The oldest member of North Eastern Railway staff at Harrogate, he had retired in 1900 after a lifetime of employment with local railways. During the mid-nineteenth century, Best was based on the York and North Midland Coke stage before moving in 1853 to become a porter at the old station opposite the Prince of Wales Hotel (which was then known as the Brunswick). In 1862 he was transferred to the present station and in about 1865, he was appointed guard. Soon after this he took up the position of ticket collector, and continued with these duties up to his retirement. When Best began work with local railways, there were three trains into Harrogate and three out of the town each day, but when he retired, the total was over 170 arriving and leaving.

Harrogate Herald

1903

16 May

St Andrew's Police Treatment Centre was officially opened on this day by Viscountess Mountgarret on a site adjacent to Harlow Carr Road. The completed project owed much to the work of Catherine Gurney OBE (1848–1930), founder of several police charities. Following the setting up of police convalescent homes and orphanages in the South of England, a convalescent home was established in the former St George's School building during January 1898. It later became known as St George's House and in 1899 the decision was taken to build a new home on an adjacent plot of land. Design work was carried out by H.S. Chorley of Leeds, and within two years, donations from police and public had raised the total amount of around £10,000. St George's House was demolished in 1976 but services at St Andrew's have been developed over the years to meet the changing nature of the police force. On 22 May 2013 HRH Prince Andrew, Duke of York, officially opened facilities that included a new physiotherapy department, gymnasium and changing room, as well as twenty-three upgraded bedrooms.

thepolicetreatmentcentres.org

1903

1 July

On this day, Alderman Charles Fortune cut the first sod at the site of Roundhill Reservoir. Along with nearby Leighton Reservoir, Roundhill is located in Colsterdale and is fed by water from High Ash Head Moor, Pott Moor, Arngill Moor and Masham Moor.

Building work was completed by Harrogate Corporation at a total cost of £568,268. After the outbreak of war in 1914, Corporation-owned land in the Colsterdale area was requisitioned by the War Office for use by the Leeds City Battalion as a training area. Accommodation used by waterworks officials during construction of the reservoir was utilised as officer accommodation, and a light railway which was built in 1901 to carry materials to the site was used to transport baggage and personal possessions. It was reported that recruits with rural skills were soon catching rabbits regularly enough to ensure a constant supply of rabbit stew from battalion cooks. During the later months of 1915, the 'Pals' were transferred to North Camp at Ripon for further training and then served overseas, before taking part in the Battle of the Somme.

The reservoir is overlooked by a curious stone structure: Carlesmoor sighting tower. This building marks the end points of a water tunnel from the reservoir to Harrogate.

nidderdaleaonb.org.uk

1903

21 September

Dramatic scenes unfolded on the afternoon of this day, while a horse-drawn omnibus was travelling from Station Square at Harrogate en route to Starbeck. After leaving the centre of Harrogate at 2.46 p.m., the omnibus had just passed the Ice House at the end of Stonefall Avenue when the middle horse of the three took fright and began to kick wildly at the top of the slope.

This sudden movement caused the driver to lose control and the bus swerved towards the right-hand kerb. As the driver attempted to steer back towards the middle of the road, his vehicle hit a lamppost and then a kerb stone. Passengers were growing increasingly alarmed and as they stood, the bus leaned further to one side. It careered forwards for another 10 yards before toppling over amid a cloud of dust, shattered glass and kicking hooves.

Ambulance men from the nearby station raced to the scene, along with police officers and doctors. The three horses were soon released from underneath the bus and taken into Harrogate for attention, and it soon became obvious that passengers on the lower deck – mainly women – had suffered more serious injury than those on the top. A number suffered broken limbs, cuts and sprains and were tended in nearby houses until specialist care could be arranged.

Abbott, Stephen G., *Starbeck: A Journey Through the Past*

1904

17 October

On this day, work got underway on a library building, using designs by H.T. Hare. It was initially intended to form a section of a huge neo-baroque 'municipal palace', complete with clock tower, on a site in Victoria Avenue. In fact, only the library was built and three-quarters of the overall cost of around £10,000 was met by the Andrew Carnegie Foundation. It was fitting that the official opening on 24 January 1906 should be performed by the Bishop of Bath and Wells, another popular Spa resort. There was no further building work on the site after that, and ground adjacent to the library was laid out as a public garden after the First World War.

It was not until April 1949 that a children's library was set up in the basement of the library building. Another notable landmark was celebrated on 4 October 2011, when HRH Prince Richard, Duke of Gloucester, cut a celebratory cake following a £3.4 million refurbishment programme. Funding from the Big Lottery and North Yorkshire County Council facilitated the creation of additional space to browse the 73,000 books on the shelves. In addition, thirty-seven public-access PCs were installed, and Wi-Fi throughout the building enabled people to use their own laptops in study areas.

harrogatenews.co.uk

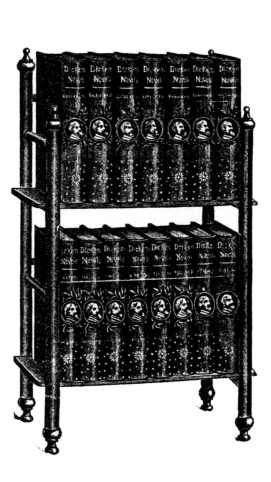

1908

5 August

On this day a great charity cricket match was staged at the ground of Harrogate Cricket Club. A feature of the first decade of the twentieth century was the number and variety of sporting events which aimed to raise funds for local charities, and this occasion was intended to give the people of Harrogate a flavour of international cricket.

One side – an 'all England XI' – was composed of tradesmen from the town who were suitably attired in white flannels, wide red braces and top hats while their opponents, a 'West Indies' team, sported flat caps. They achieved a greater degree of 'authenticity' by coating their faces, arms and hands in black boot polish.

A report in the *Harrogate Advertiser* stated:

> … At one o'clock, a procession was formed in Station Square, and, headed by the Temperance Band, proceeded to the cricket field. The weather was not at all favourable, being cold, and slight showers added to the discomfiture. Notwithstanding the adverse climatic conditions, however, there was good attendance … The Temperance Band played during the afternoon, and an entertainment was given during the interval by Mr Tim Coleman's Pierrots.

The 'All England XI' scored 113 runs and the 'West Indians' 101, while the sum of £20 was raised for the Harrogate Infirmary.

1910

2 July

On this day, peat baths were opened by the Mayor of Harrogate as an extension of the town's Royal Baths. Made from Burma teak, each bath contained 50 gallons of mineral peat, richly impregnated with iron and salts, which had been 'exposed for six or seven months before using'.

The *Harrogate Advertiser* reported:

> … There are eight baths here altogether, four entered from the ladies' corridor and four approached from the gentleman's corridor. A great saving of space has been effected by installing one needle bath between two bathrooms. An automatic shutter closing down gives privacy to each bather. It was the old custom for the bather to enter a sort of slipper bath in order to remove peat from the body. These needle baths are not only refreshing in themselves, but achieve their purpose without in the least degree calling upon the patient to exert herself or himself … The whole suite of baths are compactly designed. Everything that makes for comfort and efficiency is there. Obviously, then these baths are a great improvement. They mark a new epoch in the history of Harrogate with regard to its bathing establishments.

Blakeson, Barbara, *The Royal Pump Room Museum*

1911

22 February

On this day Harrogate's Empire Music Hall was opened, in premises which had originally accommodated a Primitive Methodist chapel (of 1871–72) on Cheltenham Parade. The church had been designed by local architect, Arthur Hiscoe, but it was a very different stylist, Thomas Holden – a puppeteer – who transformed it into a venue for entertainment. One of Holden's most prominent features was a splendid proscenium arch, beneath which a host of music hall artists performed until its closure on 10 October 1931.

A section of the Empire Buildings was adapted for commercial use, but the auditorium and stage area became derelict. Its importance to the town's heritage was recognised by Fridel Dalling-Hay, who organised a thorough programme of restoration in 1986–87. Empire Buildings became part of Pinocchio's restaurant, but near tragedy followed in the early hours of 16 September 1994, when the building was subjected to an arson attack. Sterling work by the town's fire brigade prevented total destruction and a concerted effort by restaurant staff saw the premises reopen in time for the 1994 Christmas season.

Neesam, Malcolm, *Images of England: Harrogate*

1911

12 July

At about 4 p.m. on this day, the first vehicles in the Anglo-German motor car tour of Great Britain arrived in Harrogate, at the halfway point of their rally. After reaching the borough boundary on Leeds Road, the touring cars continued along West Park, past large crowds of onlookers. Participants in the 400-strong rally included 150 guests of the British Royal Automobile Club, along with forty members of the German Imperial Motor Car Club. The idea for an Anglo-German tour of Great Britain had been first put forward by Prince Henry of Prussia, brother to the German Emperor, Wilhelm II, and trophies were donated by members of the German court as well as King George V and Queen Mary. Many of the fine rally vehicles were parked in Johnson's garage on Springfield Mount, and the nearby Hotel Majestic flew the German Imperial flag from its roof to greet Prince Henry. Overcrowding at the Majestic meant that some guests, including Sir Arthur and Lady Conan Doyle, moved to the Grand, where they were soon joined by the Earl and Countess of Brownlow, who claimed that the air would be polluted by fumes from the touring cars.

Neesam, Malcolm, *Hotel Majestic*

1911

24 July

Competitors in the *Daily Mail* Circuit of Britain Air Race landed at Harrogate during the second stage between Hendon and Edinburgh. The event was financed by Lord Northcliffe, millionaire owner of the *Daily Mail*, and prize money on offer totalled £10,000. The race had begun two days earlier at Brooklands in Surrey, when seventeen aircraft left on the 20-mile flight to Hendon Aerodrome, but the second stage, covering 343 miles, offered a more daunting prospect. Harrogate represented a compulsory stop on the northbound route and six aircraft touched down on the level expanse of Harrogate Stray between Oatlands Drive and Wetherby Road, where a large grandstand had been installed for civic dignitaries and invited guests. The first plane came into view soon after 7 a.m., and a second aircraft landed just under five minutes later, followed by a third plane, which came into view some twenty-five minutes afterwards. It was piloted by an Englishman, James Valentine (the other planes were flown by two French aviators), and he was presented with a superb silver tea service, provided by the Harrogate Chamber of Trade. A total of five aircraft reached Harrogate on 24 July, and four of these completed the five stages back to Brooklands, where James Valentine won the Entente Cordiale prize of 50 guineas from the proprietors of Perrier table water as the first Englishman to complete the course.

Wikipedia

1912

27 September

A ceremony took place on this day to mark the opening of a new school for girls, close to Pennypot Lane in Harrogate. The guest of honour was Princess Helena, Duchess of Albany, who had arrived at Harrogate station earlier in the day, where she was met by civic dignitaries including the mayor, Councillor Rowntree, members of the council and the town clerk, J. Turner Taylor. The highlight of the event came when she used a gold key to officially mark the opening of the building which had seen the laying of the foundation stone almost two years earlier, in October 1910, by Viscountess Mountgarret. During the school's first Speech Day at Queen Margaret's School, the headmistress, Miss Boddy, recalled that it was also Trafalgar Day 'and spoke of what that meant to England'.

Initially the school was part of the Woodward Corporation – an organisation set up to promote education under the Church of England – and the twelve pupils were allocated to two houses, Cantwara and Eoforwic. In 1932, Derwent and Lyminge Houses were added, but after a decline during the 1980s, the school was facing closure by 1990. During September 1990, the school was taken over by an International Trust managed by Elizabeth and Brian Martin and a move to premises at Thorpe Underwood between York and Harrogate saw it renamed Queen Ethelburga's College. (The original premises at Pennypot Lane were demolished in 1995.)

qc.org

1913

7 June

Harrogate was bathed in glorious summer sunshine on this day, as local townspeople admired a whole range of colourful decorations that had been arranged in readiness for the arrival of Sir David Burnett, Lord Mayor of London. After a four-hour journey from the capital, a special Harrogate Express pulled into its destination at 1.39 p.m., where Mayor Rowntree and the High Sheriff of Yorkshire greeted their guests. The state landau, brought specially from London, was used to carry Sir David through the streets of Harrogate to a reception at the Queen Hotel. Afterwards, an impressive procession assembled in the forecourt of the hotel with mounted police, the band of the Yorkshire Hussars and the Harrogate mace-bearer at the front. Behind came a stream of magnificent coaches, carrying civic dignitaries from many parts of the country. With appropriate musical accompaniment, the procession made its way to Crescent Gardens where large numbers of local people had gathered to watch the main business of the day. Attention then focussed on the Winter Gardens of the Royal Baths where the Lord Mayor of London delivered a speech during which he declared the annex to the Royal Pump Room open. The day's proceedings were completed with a lavish banquet for 400 invited guests at the town's Majestic Hotel.

Neesam, Malcolm, *Exclusively Harrogate*

1919

17 July

Bettys Café Tea Rooms, which grew into one of Harrogate's best-known businesses, opened its doors to the public for the first time on this day. The driving force behind the enterprise was Fritz Bützer, who began life in a remote area of rural Switzerland. Orphaned in tragic circumstances at the age of 5 in 1890, he soon showed interest and no little skill at baking, confectionery and chocolate-making. After qualifying as a baker in 1903, Fritz worked his way around Switzerland for three years before moving to Marseilles and then Paris. A further move saw him arrive in England at the age of 22, where he spent time in Bradford and several other Yorkshire towns with the trade name, 'Frederick Belmont, Chocolate Specialist'.

During 1912 he was invited to Harrogate by Farrah's, toffee makers, to demonstrate how to make smart continental chocolates, and he remained in the town between 1914 and 1918. During the early months of 1919, Fritz Bützer formed a private company and then bought and equipped premises with high-quality showcases and mirrors and a smoking room at first-floor level. Following the opening, the tea rooms became more and more popular with the upper classes and business prospered. Fritz Bützer, or Frederick Belmont as he had become known by this time, was soon seeking more space for his enterprise.

Wild, Jonathan, *Hearts, Tarts and Rascals*

1920

18 May

The first marriage in the Harrogate Synagogue took place on this day between Hyman Tankel of Glasgow and Bertha Sachs of Leeds, with Revd Eli Kahan serving as marriage secretary. He had been elected as Minister at the Jewish Synagogue some two years previously and continued to assist members of the Harrogate Congregation in their support for the religious and financial aspects of their previous synagogue, the Old Hebrew Congregation in Belgrave Street, Leeds. Cooperation between the two communities continued into the 1930s, and on 7 December 1938, a party of twenty-six girls arrived at the Harrogate District Convalescent Home, which was probably the first hostel of its type in the country. Girls aged between 10 and 16 were welcomed by members of the Leeds and Harrogate communities and they visited the synagogue during Saturday morning and Sunday afternoon. Entertainment was provided in the schoolroom by members of the Leeds Jewish Institute Dramatic Society, who received support from the Harrogate Literary and Social Union. Revd Kahan was elected as minister for life in 1935, and led the congregation for a total of thirty-five years.

Livshin, Rosalyn, *History of the Harrogate Jewish Community*

1920

28 August

This day represented an important occasion in the history of soccer in Harrogate when the town's team, Harrogate AFC, played their first match at the club's present site, then known as 'Wetherby Lane'. This Yorkshire League game resulted in a 2−1 victory over York YMCA. Initial moves to establish a first class 'Association' Town team had got underway in the early 1900s, but with the outbreak of the First World War in 1914, all fixtures were postponed and it was not until the summer of 1919 that Harrogate AFC was formed. Home matches during that season were played at the Starbeck Lane Ground and, in addition to an appearance in the English Cup (now the FA Cup), the team also won the Whitworth Cup (the senior local cup) with a 4−0 victory against Ripon City.

There was further silverware for the Sulphur and Blacks − or 'Sulphurites' as they are popularly known − on 9 May 1925, when they beat Fryston Colliery 3−1 in the West Riding County Challenge Cup at Elland Road, Leeds in front of a crowd of 2,725. More success followed in the late 1920s but sadly the club disbanded in 1932. It was during 1948 that Harrogate Hotspurs (founded in 1935) became the new Town team. Since that time, Harrogate Town have enjoyed fluctuating fortunes on the pitch, with a highlight being an extended FA Cup run in the 2012−13 season. The ground itself has also seen significant improvements with the installation of floodlights in 1982 and a cantilevered grandstand in 1990.

harrogatetownafc.com

1921

9 July

On this day the founder of the Boy Scout movement, Lord Robert Baden-Powell, visited Harrogate to officially present 'Peter's Pole' to the Clifton House School Pack, which had won the award for the best pack in the United Kingdom. A report in the *Harrogate Advertiser* stated:

> … After the salute, the 10th Harrogate pack gave the grand howl, and the Chief Scout then presented 'Peter's Pole' to the 10th Harrogate – Clifton House – Wolf Cub pack. Sixer Roper receiving it on behalf of his colleagues. The pole is named after Baden Powell's son, Peter, and is presented to the pack which gains the most marks for efficiency. Commander Dr. Laura Veale was also present.

Fluttering over the level expanse of The Stray on this occasion was a ragged Union flag which had previously been flown over Fort Ayre, at Mafeking; following the Relief of Mafeking in May 1900, it passed into the possession of a scoutmaster of the 1st Harrogate Troop.

A local scouting landmark was reached on 9 May 1999, when the 10th Harrogate (St Wilfrid's) Walsh's Own Scout Group celebrated twenty-one years of scouting at St Wilfrid's, and ninety years of scouting since the 10th Harrogate was set up at Clifton House School.

1923

1 September

On this day, the war memorial in Prospect Place was unveiled by the 6th Earl of Harewood in the presence of a distinguished company, including Princess Mary and Viscount Lascelles. Harrogate Corporation had bought land on the site of the former Prospect Gardens at a cost of £5,000 and spent a further £3,940 preparing the ground. The cost of the 75ft-high memorial, which was constructed in Portland stone, amounted to £5,500 and this sum was met by public subscription. Some fifteen months earlier, on 2 June 1922, the foundation stone had been laid by the Honourable Edward Wood (later Lord Halifax), MP for the Ripon Division.

Gilbert Ledward designed the bronze panels on the stonework. They bear inscriptions showing Britannia above a group of soldiers, with a dove of peace flying over their heads. There is also a scene of a call to arms and a list of names of all those who perished in the war.

Harrogate Advertiser

1923

29 September

On this day a service of dedication was held at the opening of a new chapel at Harrogate Ladies' College, with the Right Revd the Lord Bishop of Ripon officiating. Founded by Mr G.M. Savery in 1893 at premises on Ripon Road, the school was moved to the Oval before occupying its current site in Clarence Drive. From the outset the college placed great emphasis on religious matters, including Sunday services which were held in the main assembly hall, and initial moves to build a separate chapel were made during the early 1900s. Following the end of the First World War, detailed planning got underway and external walls were constructed with stone from the old St Mary's church. The interior of the chapel includes roof timbers and the chancel arch from St Mary's, while the wheel window includes a fragment of glass from Ypres Cathedral, which was destroyed during the First World War. In addition to its role as a religious centre, the chapel has seen regular use for staging musical events, which have often featured the fine organ designed by Abbott & Smith of Leeds.

Neesam, Malcolm, *Bygone Harrogate*

1926

8 May

This day saw the opening matches in the second round of the Davis Cup at Harrogate, where Britain took on Poland. This was the twenty-first anniversary of a tournament originally known as the International Lawn Tennis Challenge before being renamed the Davis Cup after Dwight Davis' trophy. Initially the tournament had only featured Great Britain – then known as the British Isles – and the United States of America, but by the 1920s there were over twenty nations playing regularly in the competition. The Europe Zone second-round match at Harrogate was played between Britain and Poland on a clay (shale) outdoor surface at the town's Royal Hall Gardens. In the singles matches Turnbull (Britain) beat Kleinadel (Poland) 6–1, 7–5, 6–0 while his compatriot, Wheatley, defeated his Polish opponent Czetwertynski 6–4, 6–3, 6–4. The final match score was 5–0 to Great Britain and although they reached the final of the tournament at the end of July, the British team lost by a margin of 0–5 to France.

trove.nla.gov.au

1926

14 December

A dramatic eleven-day mystery was resolved on this day when the novelist Agatha Christie was found safe and well at the Old Swan Hotel in Harrogate. Born in 1890 and brought up in Torquay, her first novel was published during 1920 with the Belgian detective, Hercule Poirot, as the main character. A highly successful career was underway when she disappeared from her Surrey home on 3 December, and fears for Christie's safety only increased when her car was discovered later the same day, perched precariously on the edge of a high chalk cliff. A widespread search by more than 1,000 police officers and civilians, as well as aircraft, found no clue as to her whereabouts and it was only when she was recognised by a banjo player at the hotel that the mystery was explained. It became clear that Agatha Christie had travelled by train to London and then Harrogate, where she had booked into the Swan Hydro, now the Old Swan Hotel, with only a small amount of luggage.

Agatha Christie never made reference to her eleven-day disappearance, and although various theories have been put forward, including difficulties in her home life, an elaborate publicity stunt and a rare medical condition, it remains unexplained. She died in 1976.

BBC News

1930

11 January

On this day Princess Mary visited Harrogate for the opening of the town's Mercer Art Gallery. A large crowd gathered to welcome the royal visitor who was met by Harrogate's mayor and mayoress, Alderman and Mrs Annakin, as well as other dignitaries, including the town clerk and the Bishop of Ripon.

After Lord Harewood had opened the new art gallery, he stated that in its first exhibition, Harrogate had a collection which did credit to the town. The official party then toured the galleries with the curator, Mr George Byers. The Princess Royal was able to view a portrait of herself, painted by J.J. Shannon, Royal Academician, and as she caught sight of *Keighley from Ilkley Moor* by J. Buxton Knight, she was heard to say, 'That is pretty'. Other paintings on display included a portrait of Edward Viscount Lascelles loaned by Lord Harewood. and several works by Turner loaned by Major Fawkes of Farnley Hall.

A report in the *Harrogate Advertiser* claimed: '… Lighting of the gallery has been the subject of the most careful consideration to ensure the most evenly distributed illumination by natural and artificial lighting and the results are considered by many experts to be highly satisfactory.'

Harrogate Advertiser

1931

3 October

Press reports on this day brought news of the death, at the age of 81, of Thomas Rochford. Affectionately known as 'Old Tom', he lived at Brunswick Cottage, West Park and was considered the leading figure among Harrogate Bath chairmen. He is credited with introducing the Coventry Cycle Chair to Harrogate; this means of transport, which combined the comfort of the Bath Chair with the pedal power of the bicycle, was popular with all age groups among both visitors and residents.

Visitors who travelled in Tom Rochford's pedal cycle included some of the best-known names of Edwardian England, such as Lord Londonderry, the Countess of Westmorland, the Duchess of Sutherland and the Duchess of Devonshire, while the singer Madam Patti hired 'Old Tom' to transport her to see the otter hunts on the banks of the River Nidd. Royal approval was given by King Edward VII, who sat in the chair and complimented 'Old Tom' on its comfort. Shortly after the end of the Boer War, Winston Churchill arranged mass rallies by what he termed the Harrogate Bathchair Artillery, with participants setting out from Pier Head to race down Parliament Street on the way to the finishing line at Fountains Abbey. Another royal customer was Princess Alix of Hesse, who was accompanied along the route by a bicycle-riding detective.

Neesam, Malcolm, *Bygone Harrogate*

1932

17 September

On this day HRH Mary, Princess Royal, performed the opening ceremony at Harrogate and District General Hospital. Patients were gradually admitted, but older premises continued to operate in conjunction with the new hospital until a new outpatient department was completed. Building costs were said to total £114,829. An increase in the number of patients treated by the various departments of the hospital resulted in the launch, during 1934, of the 'Thirty Thousand Fund' by the treasurer, Mr G.G. Stephenson. Although voluntary subscriptions to the fund fell short of the target, with a total of around £17,850, it was described as 'a very present help in time of trouble'.

Various projects were under consideration. These included improved facilities for nursing staff, a massage department and maternity and isolation blocks. By 1939, the schemes had been completed. During the previous year the hospital had received a significant increase in status when it was recognised by the Royal College of Surgeons as a training facility for house surgeons, and the outbreak of war in 1939 resulted in a rapid increase in the development of the hospital.

harrogatepeopleandplaces.info

1936

28 September

On this day, the Odeon cinema was opened on the corner of East Parade and Station Avenue at Harrogate. This single-screen venue had seating for an audience of 1,647 and was designed by Harry Weedon in the fashionable art deco style. Overall costs amounted to almost £32,000 with seating originally divided into stalls and balcony seating.

The Odeon Company began operations in 1930, when Oscar Deutsch (1893–1941) opened its first cinema with the Odeon name at Birmingham on 4 August. During the pre-war years, cinema-going increased considerably and Deutsch opened more than 250 cinemas and most of these were built in the Streamlined Moderne style, after Weedon became involved with the Odeon chain in 1934.

The dominant feature of the Odeon Harrogate's design is a central brown-brick tower, with a projecting taller 'fin' clad in biscuit-coloured faience tiles. At the top of the fin, 'cinema' is spelt out in slender lettering. Internal alterations in 1972, 1989 and 2001 added more screens and this dramatic building was awarded Grade II listed status on 24 May 1988.

modernistbritain.co.uk

1937

31 January

A major fire on this day caused the complete destruction of Harrogate's Market Building, which had been designed by Arthur Hiscoe and opened for business on 29 August 1874. The building had already survived an earlier fire on 21 March 1914, but after this latest blaze, only the clock tower was left standing.

A replacement market hall was designed by Leonard Clarke and opened in 1939, but a major redevelopment took place in the early 1990s. With funding from the National Provident Institution, a partnership between Harrogate Borough Council and Speyhawk Retail plc, Clarke created a shopping centre that reflected the design features of Palladio's Basilica at Vicenza. Architects Cullearn and Phillips of Manchester set a new market hall on the ground floor, with other floors housing a range of shops and boutiques. The premises were opened to the public on 9 November 1992.

As part of the overall development scheme, the adjacent Station Square was restyled and Queen Victoria's Monument (built to celebrate her Golden Jubilee in 1887) was cleaned and illuminated by the Borough Council.

openplaques.org

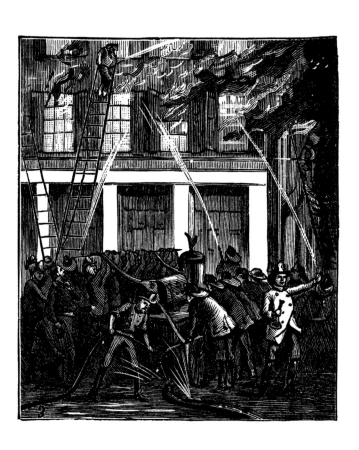

1939

17 February

On this day No. 58 (Harrogate) Squadron of the Air Defence Cadet Corps was established at Harrogate Grammar School by the Air League of the British Empire. Harrogate Grammar School had been founded in 1903 as the Municipal Secondary Day School of Harrogate, with premises in Haywra Crescent, but when Grammar School status was achieved in 1931, the number of pupils on roll had increased from an initial forty-four (in 1903) to 666, and two years later staff and pupils moved to new premises in Arthur's Avenue.

During the Second World War, many evacuees were moved to Harrogate from industrial areas and the number of pupils increased to 900. Afterwards, the squadron moved to separate premises and is no longer directly linked with the school, although some pupils continue to be active cadets within the squadron.

In recent decades the school has seen further building projects including sports facilities and music and technology areas during the 1970s, and a humanities building in the 1990s. In 2011, Harrogate Grammar School became an 'independent academy trust' with specialist status in the teaching of language and technology.

Wikipedia

1940

14 February

An article in the *Harrogate Herald* on this day notified residents that the town's Sun Pavilion would not be blacked out and a special weekly column of events at the venue was published. Its popularity among local residents was assured and the same newspaper's edition on 3 July 1940 described it as 'a miniature oasis of gaiety and pleasure in a war-ridden world'. During the late summer of 1941, morning coffee was served to a succession of well-known stage personalities, including Sybil Thorndike, Joan Cross, Margot Fonteyn and Frederick Ashton as the town's Kursaal hosted performances by the Royal Opera House Covent Garden, the Old Vic Company and Sadler's Wells Opera Company. The post-war era saw considerable change in Harrogate, with a decline in spa-related trade and the increase of exhibition and conference business, but the Sun Pavilion continued to offer a setting for taking light refreshments while listening to a band. A range of special events were held in the main pavilion and there was particular affection, among local folk, for the performances of Doris Nixon on the organ at 3 p.m. every afternoon (apart from Sundays and Mondays) and 'Old Tyme Music Hall' at the end of each week.

Harrogate Herald

1940

12 September

The only air raid on Harrogate took place on this day when a single German bomber, a Junkers 88, made a daytime attack on the Hotel Majestic. Enemy sources mistakenly believed that the building was the base for a department of the Air Ministry and three bombs were dropped by the aircraft. The first bomb failed to explode and became stuck in a fifth-floor bedroom, while a second one fell in the hotel grounds. It was the third bomb that caused considerable damage. It fell on an empty property at the corner of Ripon and Swan Roads, fracturing gas and water mains.

Soldiers searching for the unexploded device at the Hotel Majestic initially mistook it for a water tank but then, under the leadership of Captain Yates, they were able to defuse and remove it from the premises by using one of the hotel's lifts. The outer casing was salvaged and put on display to raise money for the Harrogate Spitfire Fund.

Mitchell, W.R., *Harrogate Past*

1944

19 December

Record producer, writer, musician and broadcaster Ian Stuart Colman was born in Harrogate on this day. Inheriting his family's musical background, he formed a school band, The Demons, which specialised in playing rock 'n' roll classics. After moving to Rugby for training as a draughtsman, he again set up a band, this time with fellow workers – The Cataracts.

In 1963, Stuart Colman joined The Beat Preachers and three years later he became a member of Pinkerton's Assorted Colours, who enjoyed chart success with 'Mirror Mirror'/'She Don't Care'. They were later renamed The Flying Machine and gained a gold disc with 'Smile A Little Smile for Me' in 1969.

In 1976 Colman organised a march on BBC Broadcasting House, in an attempt to persuade the BBC to play more rock music on mainstream programmes, and this led to him presenting a weekly rock 'n' roll show on BBC Radio 1. This link with Radio 1 continued until 1981, along with an Echoes series (1978–88), and his work with Shakin' Stevens and other artists saw him named 'Top Singles Producer of the Year' in 1982.

During the 1980s Stuart Colman produced albums by many of rock 'n' roll's household names including The Crickets, Phil Everly and Little Richard, as well as the Comic Relief record for 1986 – 'Livin' Doll' by Cliff Richard and The Young Ones.

In recent years he has been based in Nashville and Manhattan, with projects including scriptwriting and product management, along with studio work.

1948

1 July

Harrogate's Old Swan Hotel was officially reopened on this day after being requisitioned during the Second World War for use by the Ministry of Aircraft Production and the Ministry of Supply. First established as an eighteenth-century inn, the Swan prospered during the 1800s under the ownership of the Shutt family. Following major alterations in 1878, the Swan had become the Harrogate Hydro and some seventy years later, after its wartime role, the building was again in need of refurbishment.

Under the guidance of the general manager, Mr G.A. Wright, a series of changes and improvements were carried out during the post-war years. The establishment of a day nursery represented a distinct innovation and a further name change saw the building become the 'Old Swan'. Internal refurbishment included restoration of the Tudor-style bar, and in 1953 Mr Wright reintroduced a hornblower to greet motor coaches. He also allowed the hotel's nursery to be used as a stockroom when the International Toy Fair was staged in Harrogate. In 1977 filming took place at the 'Old Swan' for the movie *Agatha*, starring Dustin Hoffman and Vanessa Redgrave.

Neesam, Malcolm, *Bygone Harrogate*

1948

19 August

The actor Jim Carter was born in Harrogate on this day and attended the town's Ashville College before taking up law studies at the University of Sussex. A keen interest in drama saw him cut short his degree course after two years to join a theatre group at Brighton. An outstanding career as a professional actor got underway in the early 1970s with work at the Combination Theatre Company in Brighton and he later joined the Newcastle Theatre Company, where roles included Estragon in *Waiting for Godot*. During the mid-1970s he toured America with the Ken Campbell Roadshow, and in 1977 he joined the National Theatre Company to make appearances as Dom Frollo in *The Hunchback of Notre Dame* at the Cottesloe Theatre. During 1978 Jim Carter jointed the Young Vic Theatre Company, where he appeared in productions that included *Richard III* and *Bartholomew Fair*. In 1982 he met his future wife, Imelda Staunton, when they both acted in the National Theatre's revival of *Guys and Dolls* and after an interval of about fourteen years, he appeared at the same venue in *The President of an Empty Room*.

Numerous film and television roles in the last twenty years have seen Jim Carter become a household name. Film credits include *The Madness of King George* (1994), *Brassed Off* (1996) and *The Golden Compass* (2007), while television appearances include *Cracker* (1994), *Midsomer Murders* (2004) and *Cranford* (2007). He is probably best known, though, for his role as Carson in *Downton Abbey*.

Wikipedia

1949

18 July

On this day Harrogate's Tewit Well was awarded Grade II*
listed building status. Discovered in 1571 by William Slingsby,
it represented the first of Harrogate's chalybeate springs
and is considered to be the oldest spa in England. In 1841,
the town's Improvement Commissioners constructed the new
Royal Pump Room in Crown Place and moved the Sulphur
Well Temple to the Tewit Well. In view of its exposed location
on The Stray, the commissioners decided to complete a wall
inside the twelve Tuscan columns of the temple and to build a
cottage to accommodate the well attendant. (Design work for
this single-storey property was completed by the architect, Isaac
Thomas Shutt.)

After some four centuries of continuous use by members of
the public, the Tewit Well had fallen into disrepair by the early
1970s. In recent years, however, restoration work has included
removal of the internal wall and installation of a concrete cover
over the top of the well.

britishlistedbuildings.co.uk

1950

2 September

On this day, a special gala day took place in Harrogate during the town's 'Fete and Gala Carnival'. Events got underway at 1.30 p.m., with a carnival procession through the streets and a whole range of activities during the rest of the day, including a motorcycle gymkhana, 'keep fit' displays and a 'sensational high diving and comedy trampolinists aqua show of great perfection' by the Safto brothers.

Large crowds also gathered for the crowning of the town's 'Floral Queen'. During the summer, rounds had been held to eliminate contestants and the final was held in the Sun Pavilion on 7 August. BBC producer Barney Colehan acted as chairman when ten girls were interviewed by a panel of five and the title of 'Floral Queen' was eventually awarded to 14-year-old Audrey Nathan.

Harrogate's mayoress, Mrs C.E. Whiteley, crowned the Floral Queen at 2.20 p.m. in the Floral Gardens, and her procession then moved through the town's main streets to reach the Yorkshire Show Ground.

Harrogate Advertiser

1954

17 November

Professor John Robert Wilkinson was born on this day in Harrogate and educated at the town's Ashville College (1965–72) before completing medical studies at Edinburgh University. After entering general practice in England he chose to pursue a career in public health and gained relevant academic and professional qualifications at northern universities. In 2000 he was appointed as the first director of the Northern and Yorkshire Public Health Observatory and developed the organisation, with successful bids to deliver the National Library for Public Health, the National Observatory for Learning Difficulties and a number of IT-based projects.

During 2010 the role of cancer registry director and medical director was added to his portfolio. This followed work during the 1990s as lead commissioner for cancer services in Yorkshire, and an important contribution to developing bone-marrow services within the county. Professor Wilkinson has contributed more than sixty articles to medical journals, mainly in the areas of information and intelligence, and as well as holding a substantive professorial post with Durham University, he is also visiting professor at Leeds and Teesside universities.

twri.org.uk

1957

9 July

The 100th Great Yorkshire Show opened at the showground in Harrogate on this day. Founded as an annual event in 1838, the event was organised by the Yorkshire Agricultural Society at Barrack Yard, Fulford, '… to hold an Annual Meeting for the Exhibition of Farming Stock, Implements etc. … and for the General Promotion of Agriculture.' The original scheme included plans to change the venue on an annual basis, and it was staged in Leeds, Northallerton and Hull before moving back to York in 1842 when paying customers totalled 6,044. Until 1950, the three-day annual event was staged at different locations in Yorkshire, with cancellations during both world wars, but from 1951, when attendance figures amounted 54,000, it has taken place at the permanent showground in Harrogate.

On the second day of the show in 1957 (10 July), HM Queen Elizabeth II and Prince Phillip paid a visit, during which the Canadian Mounted Police gave a demonstration of synchronised riding. Following a showjumping competition, the royal couple presented prizes to the winners and walked around the perimeter to talk to the assembled crowds.

yorkshirefilmarchive.com

1959

13 September

On this day Starbeck motive power depot, situated in the fork of the Knaresborough and Leeds lines south of Starbeck station, was closed. It had opened in 1857 as a brick-built two-road shed, and was subsequently lengthened on four occasions in 1864, 1877, 1888 and 1889, which made it one of the longest depots in the country. Its facilities included a turntable.

The growth in railway facilities at Starbeck led to a rapid increase in the local population, from 800 in 1889, to 5,000 in 1904. By 1882 Starbeck was dealing with thirty-five passenger and eighty-five goods trains daily, along with many shunting operations, and it was estimated that the railway was responsible for the livelihoods of as many as 75 per cent of local residents.

By the 1950s the railway centre at Starbeck had slipped into decline. The Pateley Bridge branch line closed to passengers on 31 March 1951, and after the Crimple low viaduct was found to be unsafe and beyond repair, the Pannal to Starbeck line closed to passenger traffic on 12 September and goods trains on 7 October 1951. During the 1950s, the roof of the motive power building was removed and in 1956 the building was truncated and a flat roof and brick screen installed. Following closure, the shed was finally demolished in 1962.

Griffiths, Roger, and Smith, Paul, *Directory of British Engine Sheds*

1963

8 March

A poster at the Royal Hall for this day advertised 'Dancing for Teens and Twenties with the Recording Stars of "Please Please Me", the Sensational Beatles together with Harrogate's most popular groups – Barry Corbett and his Mustangs along with The Chinchillas and The Apaches'. Tickets for the event, which lasted from 8 p.m. to 1 a.m., cost 10*s* 6*d* (53p). Members of the local groups recall the casual manner of the Beatles on their arrival at the theatre, each carrying their own gear and accompanied by a single roadie. Wearing black leather coats, they found time to pause and share a joke about all the amps on the stage. Their stage act was said to be quite different from the usual sounds heard at the Royal Hall. Dressed in dark suits with velvet collars, they performed hard-driving Chuck Berry-style R & B and old rock 'n' roll, as well as their own number, 'Please Please Me', which had just reached No. 1 in the charts. Members of the audience dashed to the front of the stage, where they gazed in amazement as the Beatles performed two thirty-minute spots. Beatlemania had not yet gripped the nation, and at this early point – at the start of their fame – they received £50, while Brian Epstein was paid £25.

'Dancing for Teens and Twenties', 1963 poster

1963

2 September

On this day, Harrogate Rugby Union Football Club celebrated the opening of a new clubhouse at their Claro Road ground. The club's origins date back to 1871, when Harrogate Football Club was formed and their first match, played on an area now known as the West Park Stray, resulted in defeat to a Leeds team. Although the home side fielded sixteen players to Leeds' eleven, the visitors scored 1 goal and 5 touchdowns in response to Harrogate's 1 touchdown.

Some four years later came a move to Dragon Fields, and in 1896, the club transferred to its Claro Road premises. International opposition in the form of Canada featured in a match in 1903, with victory for the visitors by 5–0, and on 22 April 1905, Harrogate won the Yorkshire Cup for the first time with a score line of 7–5 against Wakefield Balne Lane.

In 1914, Harrogate FC became a soccer club, and rugby continued as Harrogate Old Boys. In 1923, Harrogate RUFC reformed and 1936 saw an amalgamation of the two clubs. (There was a further merger with Harrogate Georgians in 1957.)

The formation of leagues in 1987 saw the club placed in North 1 and, after gaining promotion to the third tier for the 1994–95 season, Harrogate RUFC remained there for thirteen successive years. During this period, the club's most successful season was 2001–02, when they finished fourth in the league, won the Yorkshire Cup and, as Yorkshire representatives, won the national 7-a-side competition.

pitchero.com

1964

19 October

Adam Pearson, a major figure in business and sporting circles in Yorkshire and the Midlands, was born in Harrogate on this day. He came to prominence during 2001 after rescuing Hull City AFC from the brink of administration and then, in his post as chairman, he played a leading role in guiding the club to successive promotions. He left Hull in 2007 after selling the club to a new owner, Russell Bartlett, and took up a similar post with Derby County FC.

Pearson returned to the Hull club, at Bartlett's request, in November 2009, when the Tigers were again in serious financial difficulties. He played a key role in negotiating a deal that saved Hull City for a second time. On this occasion it was Assem and Ehab Allam who saved the club from a threatened winding-up order, with a £21 million overnight investment. Adam Pearson was relieved of his post at Hull City, following the dismissal of the manager, Nick Barmby.

During July 2011 he secured ownership of Hull FC Super League (rugby team) and recently launched Pro Sports Recruitment – 'a search facility for sports professionals and organisations'.

Hull Daily Mail

1971

10 June

British film, television and stage actor Michael Rennie died in Harrogate on this day, while visiting his mother after the death of his brother. Born at Idle, near Bradford, on 25 August 1909, Michael, then known as Eric Alexander Rennie, had a number of jobs before turning to an acting career with a part in Alfred Hitchcock's film *Secret Agent* in 1936. He had a number of other minor roles during the late 1930s, before landing leading parts in films such as *Tower of Terror*, which was released in December 1941.

Between May 1941 and May 1944, Michael Rennie served with the RAF Volunteer Reserve, and after hostilities ended in 1945, his film career resumed, with appearances along with Margaret Lockwood in *I'll Be Your Sweetheart* and *The Wicked Lady*. His most frequent co-star, however, was Jean Simmons and together they appeared in two Twentieth Century Fox epics: *Caesar and Cleopatra* (1945) and *Desiree* (1954).

In 1959, Michael Rennie became a popular figure on television, with roles such as Harry Lime in *The Third Man*. In the early 1960s he made his only Broadway appearance in *Mary, Mary* playing Dirk Winston, a fading film star. He eventually moved to Switzerland, after making guest appearances in two films. Following his death in Harrogate, Michael Rennie's ashes were interred in the town's Harlow Hill Cemetery.

findagrave.com

1973

30 June

Cricket history was made in Harrogate on this day, when Durham became the first minor county club to defeat a first-class side in the Gillette Cup competition. Yorkshire batted first, and after losing their first wicket for only 18 runs, they struggled at 49 for 5 before Colin Johnson hit 44 to help them towards a more respectable score of 121–8. The final 2 wickets added only 14 runs to leave Yorkshire all out for 135, and in their reply Durham reached 57 runs before losing their first wicket. Another wicket followed after just 5 more runs were added to the total, but the minor county side battled through to complete an unexpected victory by 5 wickets.

Interest was added by the appearance of Alan Old, holder of 16 England caps at fly half for England's rugby team, in the Durham side while his brother Chris played for Yorkshire. Before their promotion to first-class county status in 1991, Durham won the Minor County Championship nine times (between 1900 and 1984) and created a record of sixty-five minor county matches without defeat.

Northern Echo

1975

21 July

Simon Easterby, Irish international rugby union player, was born in Harrogate on this day. After an education at Ampleforth College in North Yorkshire, he pursued a career in rugby with Leeds Carnegie (1998–1999) before moving to the Welsh clubs Llanelli (1999–2003) and Scarlets (2003–2010). Standing 1.93m (6ft 4in) tall and weighing 100kg (15st 10lb), his performances as a flanker (in the back row of the scrum) brought international recognition in 2000 with an appearance in the Six Nations victory over Scotland at Lansdowne Road, and he played in the remaining matches of that season's Six Nations competition.

After a lengthy lay-off due to injury, Easterby returned for the match against Scotland in September 2001, and in 2002 he featured in the first ten of Ireland's matches (with eight in the starting line-up). During the next few years he was virtually ever-present for Ireland, and gained a total of 65 caps whilst scoring 40 points, until he retired from international rugby in 2008. He had also played a major part in the 2005 British Lions tour of New Zealand.

In August 2010, Simon Easterby was forced to end his playing career through injury, and he then took on a coaching role with Scarlets. This led to his appointment in June 2012 as head coach for the club.

scarlets.co.uk

1982

17 February

Two youths were stabbed and windows were broken in a town-centre bar when violence broke out during an anti-National Front demonstration at Harrogate. One of the youths was stabbed in the hand and the other received hospital treatment for a minor back wound. A television cameraman was also attacked during the demonstration, during which – according to a police spokesman – six people were arrested for alleged offences of criminal damage and public disorder. Demonstrators had gathered outside the Harrogate College of Further Education in Haywra Street to call for the resignation of politics lecturer Andrew Brons. They moved off through the town centre to hold a meeting on West Park Stray. Meanwhile, Mr Brons completed his class at the college and was driven away by a supporter, while a group of 100 National Front supporters staged a counter-demonstration. A total of around 500 police officers from many areas of Yorkshire kept the two groups apart.

Harrogate Advertiser

1982

23 March

A Harrogate school was at the centre of dramatic events on this day, as pupils were evacuated from their classrooms and army bomb disposal experts rushed 30 miles from their base at Catterick. Police officers sealed off Beckwithshaw Primary School on Otley Road after members of the teaching staff had alerted them about a suspected bomb. Earlier that morning, the school's head teacher, Mrs Jenny Gristwood, was leading a group of thirteen pupils on a nature walk in nearby Moor Park. Several 10-year-old boys at the rear of the party spotted an unidentified object among grass at the side of the pathway and drew their teacher's attention to the 9in-long cylinder, with fins at one end. It seemed harmless enough and was carried back on the half-mile return route to school, where it was placed in the school kitchen while pupils examined relevant history books for clues about its identity. Lingering doubts about the object's safety led to immediate evacuation of the 118-year-old school building while experts made a close examination. They determined that it was in fact a mortar smoke bomb, a relic of tank manoeuvres during the Second World War. It had been fired and was taken away to be destroyed, while staff and pupils pondered the wisdom of not handling suspicious objects.

Harrogate Advertiser

1982

26 March

On this day, HRH Prince Philip, Duke of Edinburgh, made a two and a half hours-long visit to the Harrogate International Centre. Arriving a few minutes ahead of schedule in bright sunshine, he was met by the official party, which included the building's architect and Harrogate's mayor and mayoress, Councillor and Mrs Frank Thackray. After signing the visitors' book, Prince Philip called at the centre's reception desk and, after spotting the public address system, asked the receptionist '… is that where you announce the train now standing at Platform 4?'

From the ground floor, the official party made their way up a spiral ramp (made from the longest length of unbroken concrete in the country) and into the 2,000-seater auditorium, before inspecting the maze of lighting and sound systems in the roof space. After a private lunch at the Centre, the Duke of Edinburgh left for a visit to York University.

Joe Bentley, one of the architects of the building, reported that HRH had told him that he considered it to be a very advanced building and one which impressed him greatly.

Harrogate Advertiser

1982

24 April

The 27th Eurovision Song Contest was held on this day at Harrogate International Centre, with entries from eighteen different countries. Host for the evening's proceedings was Jan Leeming, and media coverage was provided for United Kingdom audiences by Terry Wogan (BBC1) and Ray Moore (BBC Radio 2). During the interval, images were shown from locations in Yorkshire, and following the voting process by juries in each of the competing countries, the Germany entry was declared the winner, with a total of 161 points. Nicole, the German contestant, was last to perform and her song 'Ein Bischen Frieden' ('A Little Peace') held a considerable lead for almost all of the voting to end with a margin of 21 points over the entry from Israel. The United Kingdom's entry, 'One Step Further' by Bardo, gained 76 points to achieve seventh place. The event was brought to a rousing finale as Nicole performed her winning song in English, French and Dutch.

Wikipedia

1982

17 September

On this day a roller ski event was staged in Harrogate. It was claimed to be the first roller ski event held in Britain, and arrangements were made by the British Ski Federation and local cross-country ski instructor, Eric Woolley, with the expressed intention of publicising cross-country skiing. Harrogate Public Works Committee had earlier given permission for closure of streets that formed the race circuit (Cambridge Street, James Street and Station Square). At this meeting, Councillor Michael Laycock claimed that it was unfair to local residents that the streets should be closed. Councillor Freddie Rotherham retorted that they were lucky not to have a motorcycle race around the streets, like Scarborough.

The *Harrogate Advertiser* reported that international rider, Mick Goode, won the men's 6km race in a time of sixteen minutes fifty seconds, while 17-year-old David Gilmore from Harrogate triumphed in the junior men's race. Heather Woolley, UK ladies' champion and wife of the event organiser, was a convincing winner of the ladies' 3.6km event.

Although the sport was new to the United Kingdom, it is said to be fairly common on the Continent and in Scandinavia, where it was used by cross-country skiers for training when there was no snow.

Harrogate Advertiser

1998

3 August

On this day, the Army Foundation College was opened in Uniacke Barracks on Penny Pot Lane in Harrogate. The base had previously been in continuous use from 1947 to 1996 to provide military training and vocational education, during which time it was known as the Army Apprentices School from 1947 to 1966 and the Army Apprentices College between 1966 and 1996.

Penny Pot Lane probably derives its name from Penny Pot House, former home of the Burnell family of Fewston, which was located beside the roadway (although local folklore suggests that during the First World War, soldiers marched from their camp to a local farm where they obtained ale for 'a penny a pot').

After earlier use by the 9th Field Training Regiment, Royal Artillery and the 116th General Hospital of the United States Army, the Army Apprentices School moved into Uniacke and probably also Hildebrande Barracks in 1947. Uniacke Barracks derives its name from Lieutenant General Sir Herbert Uniacke, an artillery officer, and Hildebrand Barracks from Brigadier General Arthur Blois Ross Hildebrand, a signals officer.

In recent times the base has 1,300 soldiers, training under 500 permanent staff. Its motto is 'Trust, Courage, Team Spirit'.

Wikipedia

1998

10 December

Queen Elizabeth II and the Duke of Edinburgh visited several locations in the Harrogate area on this day. In addition to engagements at Harrogate Theatre, the Northern Police Convalescent Home in St Andrews (to mark its centenary) and Harrogate District Hospital (in celebration of its completion), the royal couple also opened the restored Sun Pavilion in Valley Gardens and spent time at one of the town's oldest industrial premises – Farrah's toffee factory. The business was established in 1840 by John Farrah, whose 'Original Harrogate Toffee' was intended to remove from the palate the putrid taste of the town's sulphur water, which had become famous for its healing properties. The toffee's unique texture and flavour is said to be derived from three different types of sugar, proper butter and a hint of lemon, and it is still made in copper pans before being packaged in blue and silver embossed tins. Following John Farrah's retirement in the early 1900s, the business was operated first by the Armitage and then the Waddington families. It was saved from closure in 1997 by father and son partnership Gary and Peter Marston.

farrahs.com

2008

22 January

HRH Charles, Prince of Wales, Patron of the Theatre Trust, formally reopened Harrogate's Royal Hall as part of the main event of a three-day grand opening. During the ceremony he had likened the hall to 'an elegant and once lovely old lady who had fallen on hard times … but after her makeover, I see she has been taken back in time to the beauty and splendour of her youth. The result is simply breathtaking.'

Following its opening as the Kursaal in 1903, this magnificent venue was an integral part of taking the 'cure' during the town's heyday as a spa resort. The building's interior was sufficiently flexible to stage concerts, tea dances and other social gatherings by day, as well as music hall performances and glittering balls in the evenings. Performers there have included the London Philharmonic, the dancer Anna Pavlova, Petula Clark and the Beatles, but by 2002, chemical salts in the building had begun to erode sections of concrete and safety concerns resulted in its closure.

In addition to grants from the Heritage Lottery Fund and Harrogate Council, a further £2.7 million was provided by members of the public through the Royal Hall Restoration Fund, and the completed project totalled £10.7 million. A further development saw the theatre trust board agree to take over the running of the Grade II* listed building from the town council in January 2012.

Quin, Stuart, *Kursaal: A History of Harrogate's Royal Hall*

2010

12 April

It was announced that Elizabeth Balmforth had been appointed as head gardener at Harlow Carr Gardens, in Harrogate. She also became the youngest and indeed first female curator in the history of the Royal Horticultural Society.

Harlow Carr was first opened in 1946, when the Northern Horticultural Society leased 10.5 hectares of mixed woodland, pasture and arable land from Harrogate Corporation. Four years later, the botanical gardens were established as a trial ground for observing the growth of plants in the Northern Hemisphere. In 2001, the Royal Horticultural Society merged with the Northern Horticultural Society and Harlow Carr, one of just four RHS gardens in the country, represented the Society's northernmost setting. Recent years have seen the regeneration of woodland areas, the addition of themed willow sculptures to annual meadows and the redesigning of main borders. Elizabeth Balmforth, who had been based at Harlow Carr for six years before her promotion to head gardener, included among her future plans improved links between the east and west sides of the gardens.

The Press

2012

12 July

The death occurred of Mehroo Jehangir, who was born in Bombay but spent most of her life in Harrogate, where she followed the example of her mother Lady Bomanji and became affectionately known as 'Lady Harrogate'. Although her age was kept secret, she was in her 90s when she died and remained strong-willed and active until the end, as shown when she hosted a dinner party for fourteen guests in celebration of HM Queen Elizabeth II's Diamond Jubilee.

Following the death of Mrs Jehangir's husband during an air raid in London, she and her mother moved to Harrogate, where they became deeply involved in many aspects of town life. This support for local organisations continued after her mother's death: Mehroo Jehangir became a patron of the Women of the North, vice-president of the Harrogate Festival of Arts and Sciences, president of the Harrogate Friendship Club and president of the Friends of Harrogate. Her presidency of the Harrogate branch of St John Ambulance was marked with a decoration by the organisation at its London headquarters in 1988.

Yorkshire Post

2012

28 July

A dramatic feature of the 2012 Summer Olympics and Paralympics in London, which opened on this day, was the cauldron which had been manufactured amid great secrecy by Harrogate-based firm Stage One. British designer Thomas Heatherwick was chosen to create the cauldron and explained that he intended it to serve as a focal point, like an altar in a church, which would symbolise 'the coming together in peace of 204 nations for two weeks of sporting competition … a representation of the extraordinary, albeit transitory, togetherness that the Olympic Games symbolise.' Following some two months of preparatory work, production got underway in the early days of 2012 with the manufacturing of individual 3mm-thick petals, hand beaten from copper sheeting and polished by skilled craftsmen. Each petal was inscribed with the name of the competing country and 'The XXX Olympiad – London 2012'. Three complete sets were made – one for the Olympics, one for the Paralympic cauldron, and another for rehearsals and testing. Strict secrecy was maintained during construction and testing at Stage One's workshop before the cauldron was installed at the centre of the Olympic Stadium overnight on 10 June 2012, in readiness for the dramatic opening ceremony.

Wikipedia

2013

10 July

A coroner's court, held at Harrogate Magistrates' Court, gave a ruling on a treasure trove found by metal detector enthusiasts at a site close to Busks Farm near Middleham. Items uncovered on 16–17 April 2011 included a gold coin, a gold pommel, a copper alloy mount, an iron sword and dagger, a copper alloy pommel and three copper alloy hooks that were believed to be from an Anglo-Saxon grave. Deputy coroner Geoff Fell heard that not all items were recorded with the Finds Liaison Officer immediately and called for five silver coins that were still missing to be returned. He concluded:

> I am recording a verdict that all items found were treasure, either because of their worth or because of their association with other items. Whoever had the silver coins – if he does not have them he would be well advised to tell whoever does have them to send them to the British Museum.

Northern Echo

2013

12 September

Preparations for staging the Yorkshire leg of the Tour de France in July 2014 moved a step forward when it was announced in the *Harrogate Advertiser* that Harrogate Borough Council was applying for the Stray Act to be suspended in order to allow the open space to be used when Harrogate features in both of the opening stages of the race. The 1985 Act requires the 200-acre Stray to remain unenclosed and unbuilt on as an open space for use by members of the public, but considerable amounts of space would be needed for the public as well as media outlets, competitors and their vehicles. A spokesperson for Harrogate Borough Council said: 'We are applying to the Communities and Local Government Secretary, Eric Pickles, to see if we can suspend the Act. We are seeking dispensation and hope Mr Pickles will be supportive of our request.'

Following the success of London 2012's 70,000-strong contingent of Games Makers, several thousand volunteers, dubbed Le Tour Makers, have already been recruited to perform a range of roles, which range from staffing information desks and distributing uniforms to providing medical support.

Harrogate Advertiser

Bibliography

Books

Abbott, Stephen G., *Starbeck: A Journey Through the Past* (Harrogate: Stephen G. Abbott, 2004)

Bebb, Prudence, *Life in Regency Harrogate* (William Sessions Ltd, 1995)

Blakeson, Barbara, *The Royal Pump Room Museum* (Harrogate: Harrogate Museums, 1993)

Grainge, William, *The History and Topology of Harrogate and the Forest of Knaresborough* (1871)

Griffiths, Roger and Smith, Paul, *Directory of British Engine Sheds and Principal Locomotive Serving Points, Vol.2: North Midlands, Northern England and Scotland* (Shepperton: Oxford Publishing Co., 2000)

Livshin, Rosalyn D., *History of the Harrogate Jewish Community* (Leeds: Leeds University Press, 1995)

Mitchell, W.R., *Harrogate Past* (Chichester: Phillimore, 2001)

Neesam, Malcolm, *Bygone Harrogate* (Derby: Breedon Books, 1999)

Neesam, Malcolm, *Exclusively Harrogate* (Otley: Smith Settle, 1989)

Neesam, Malcolm, *Harrogate Great Chronicle, 1332–1841* (Lancaster: Carnegie Publishing, 2005)

Neesam, Malcolm, *Hotel Majestic* (Morely: Paramount Hotels, 2000)

Neesam, Malcolm, *Images of England: Harrogate* (Stroud: Tempus Publishing, 1995)

Quin, Stuart (ed.), *Kursaal: A History of Harrogate's Royal Hall* (Harrogate: Harrogate International Centre, 2008)

Smith, Roly, *Harrogate: A History and Celebration* (Salisbury: Francis Frith, 2012)

St Wilfrid's Church, Harrogate guidebook

Walker, Harold Hyde, *History of Harrogate under the Improvement Commissioners 1841–1884* (Harrogate: Manor Place Press, 1986)

Wild, Jonathan, *Hearts, Tarts and Rascals: The Story of Bettys* (Harrogate: Bettys & Taylors Group, 2010)

Newspapers and Magazines

Golf magazine (London: 1890–1899)

Harrogate Advertiser (1918–)

Harrogate Herald (1847–1984)

Hull Daily Mail (1886–)

Leeds Mercury (1767–1901)

Northern Echo (1870–)

The Press (2006–)

Yorkshire Post (1883–)

Internet Sources

'2012 Summer Olympics and Paralympics Cauldron' (Wikipedia, 2013): en.wikipedia.org/wiki/2012_Summer_Olympics_and_Paralympics_cauldron

'A History of the Hotel and Harrogate' (White Hart Hotel and Conference Centre, 2013): whitehart.net/the-hotel/

'Agatha Christie's Harrogate Mystery' (BBC News, 2009): news.bbc.co.uk/local/york/hi/people_and_places/history/ newsid_8393000/8393552.stm

'Army Foundation College' (Wikipedia, 2013): en.wikipedia.org/wiki/Army_Foundation_College

'Charity History' (The Police Treatment Centres, 2013): thepolicetreatmentcentres.org/en/cat/charity-history.aspx

'Charles Hull' (Wikipedia, 2013): en.wikipedia.org/wiki/Charles_Hull

'Club History' (Harrogate Rugby, 2013): pitchero.com/clubs/harrogaterugby/a/history-7630.html

'Club History: Harrogate Town AFC' by Harrison, Phil (Harrogate Town AFC, 2013): harrogatetownafc.com/club/about-us/club-history/

'Club History: The History of Harrogate Cricket Club' (Harrogate Cricket Club, 2013): pitchero.com/clubs/harrogatecricketclub/a/club-history-23324.html

'CTC history timeline' (Cyclists Touring Club): ctc.org.uk/about-ctc/history/ctc-history-timeline

'Daily Mail Circuit of Britain Air Race' (Wikipedia, 2013):
en.wikipedia.org/wiki/Daily_Mail_Circuit_of_Britain_Air_Race

'Davis Cup: Britain wins singles' (*Brisbane Courier*, 1926):
trove.nla.gov.au/ndp/del/page/1635850

'Donald Bell's Victoria Cross raises £210,000' (BBC News, 2010):
news.bbc.co.uk/local/york/hi/people_and_places/history/
newsid_9227000/9227719.stm

'Eurovision Song Contest 1982' (Wikipedia, 2013):
en.wikipedia.org/wiki/Eurovision_Song_Contest_1982

'Farrah's History' (Farrah's, 2011):
farrahs.com/history.php

Friends of Valley Gardens (2013):
friendsofvalleygardens.co.uk/

'Great Yorkshire Show 1957' (Yorkshire Film Archive, 2011):
yorkshirefilmarchive.com/film/great-yorkshire-show-1957

'Harrogate Grammar School' (Wikipedia, 2013):
en.wikipedia.org/wiki/Harrogate_Grammar_School

'Harrogate Library gets a royal opening' (*Harrogate News*, 2011):
harrogate-news.co.uk/2011/10/04/harrogate-library-royal-opening

'Harrogate' (Open Plaques):
openplaques.org/places/gb/areas/harrogate

'Harrogate Theatre celebrates its 110th anniversary' (BBC News, 2010):
news.bbc.co.uk/local/york/hi/people_and_places/arts_and_culture/
newsid_8453000/8453150.stm

'Historical Harrogate Music' (Harrogate Band, 2013):
harrogateband.org/hbhist.htm

'History of Grove House' by Hartmann, W.A.C. (West Cornwall Province RAOB):
west_cornwall_raob.tripod.com/homepage/id17.html

'History of the Cairn' (The Cairn Hotel, 2013):
strathmorehotels.com/Cairn+Hotel/History/

'Jim Carter (actor)' (Wikipedia, 2013):
en.wikipedia.org/wiki/Jim_Carter_(actor)

'Michael Rennie' by Benson, Kit and Benson, Morgan (findagrave.com, 2002):
findagrave.com/cgi-bin/fg.cgi?page=gr&GRid=6440535

Nidderdale Area of Outstanding Natural Beauty (2013):
nidderdaleaonb.org.uk

'Obituary: Maurice Leyland' by Preston, Norman (ed.)
in *Wisden Cricketer's Almanack 1968*:
espncricinfo.com/wisdenalmanack/content/story/155454.html

'Odeon Cinema Harrogate' by Coltman, Richard (Modernist Britain, 2013):
http://www.modernistbritain.co.uk/post/building/
Odeon+Cinema+Harrogate/

'Our History' (Queen Ethelburga's Collegiate, 2013):
qe.org/history

'Professor John Wilkinson' (TWRI Policy and Research, 2013):
twri.org.uk/twri-staff/professor-john-wilkinson

'Simon Easterby' (Scarlets, 2013):
scarlets.co.uk/eng/rugby/4079.php

'Stuart Colman: It's Rock 'n' Roll' (Radio Rewind):
radiorewind.co.uk/radio1/stuart_colman_page.htm

'Tewit Well, Harrogate' (British Listed Buildings, 2013):
britishlistedbuildings.co.uk/en-329968-tewit-well-north-yorkshire

'The Harrogate Underground' by Davison, Phill (BBC News, 2008):
bbc.co.uk/northyorkshire/content/articles/2008/02/07/harrogate_
tunnel_feature.shtml

'The Knaresborough Forest Boundary Stones' by RWH
(Yorkshire Milestones, 2013):
mileston.echoechoplus.com/all-about-waymarkers/
boundary-markers/100-the-knaresborough-forest-boundary-stones.html

'The Queen of the Wells' (2003) Unnetie Project Site. North Yorkshire County Council:
northyorks.gov.uk/unnetie/storyboards/harrogate_spa/queen_of_the_
wells.cfm (Accessed 15 October 2013)

'The Story of a Hospital: The History of the Harrogate and District General
Hospital' by Edgecombe, Wilfrid (Harrogate People and Places, 2005):
harrogatepeopleandplaces.info/publications/generalhospital/19th.htm

'Thomas Thrush, the Warrior Turned Christian' (1844), *The Advocate of Peace*
(1837–1845), Vol.v, No.14, pp.157–160:
jstor.org

Also from The History Press

YORKSHIRE

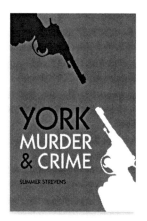

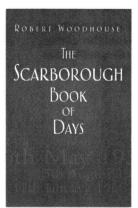

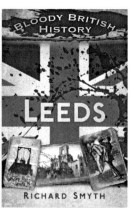

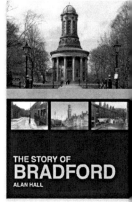

Find these titles and more at
www.thehistorypress.co.uk

Also from The History Press

HAUNTED

This series is sure to petrify everyone interested in the ghostly history of their hometown. Containing a terrifying collection of spine-chilling tales, from spooky sightings in pubs and theatres to paranormal investigations in cinemas and private homes, each book in the series is guaranteed to appeal to both serious ghost hunters and those who simply fancy a fright.

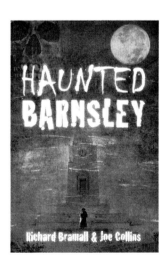

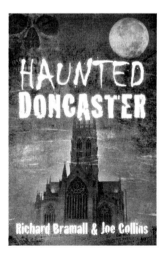

Find these titles and more at
www.thehistorypress.co.uk

Also from The History Press

MURDER & CRIME

This series brings together numerous murderous tales from history. Featuring cases of infanticide, drowning, shooting and stabbing, amongst many other chilling killings, these well-illustrated and enthralling books will appeal to everyone interested in true crime and the shadier side of their hometown's past.

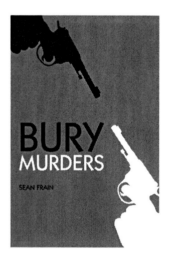

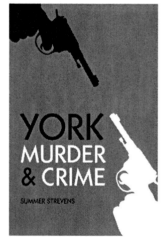

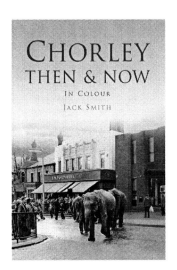
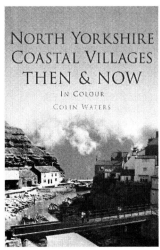

Lightning Source UK Ltd.
Milton Keynes UK
UKOW05f1927160514

231812UK00001B/7/P